Duden

Einfach klasse in

Englisch

Wissen • Üben • Testen

6. Klasse

2., neu bearbeitete und erweiterte Auflage

Dudenverlag
Mannheim • Leipzig • Wien • Zürich

Bibliografische Information der Deutschen Nationalbibliothek
Die Deutsche Nationalbibliothek verzeichnet diese Publikation in der Deutschen Nationalbibliografie; detaillierte bibliografische Daten sind im Internet über http://dnb.ddb.de abrufbar.

 D C B A

Redaktionelle Leitung Martin Bergmann
Redaktion Anika Donner, Martin Fruhstorfer
Autorinnen Birgit Hock, Petra Nagel, Annette Schomber, Linda Strehl
Sprecher Alison Ripier, Michael Shiels

Herstellung Annette Scheerer
Layout Horst Bachmann
Illustration Carmen Strzelecki
Umschlaggestaltung WohlgemuthPartners, Bremen
Umschlagabbildung Getty Images

Satz Katrin Kleinschrot, Stuttgart
Druck und Bindung Offizin Andersen Nexö Leipzig GmbH
Printed in Germany

ISBN 978-3-411-72142-9

Inhaltsverzeichnis

1 Adjektive und Adverbien

2 Modale Hilfsverben

3 Vergangenheit

4 Zukunft

INHALT

5 Der Satz

6 Fragen

7 Englisch lernen

INHALT

1 Adjektive und Adverbien

1.1 Adjektive

Adjektive *(adjectives)* beschreiben Lebewesen, Dinge oder Ereignisse näher. Mit ihnen kannst du angeben, *wie* jemand oder etwas ist.

Größe: big, tall (Menschen), small
Farbe: blue, brown, red, green
Eigenschaft: crazy, intelligent, stupid, nice

Die Steigerung von Adjektiven

Mithilfe von Adjektiven kann man Menschen und Dinge vergleichen.
Dazu benötigt man Steigerungsformen: den Komparativ (Vergleichsstufe) und den Superlativ (Höchststufe). Man steigert:
Positiv (Grundstufe) → Komparativ → Superlativ.

Andy is tall. Steven is taller. But Rick is the tallest boy.

Es gibt zwei Formen der Steigerung:
Die Steigerung mit ***-er*** und ***-est*** gilt für
- einsilbige Adjektive,
- zweisilbige Adjektive, die auf *-y* enden.

cheap → cheaper → cheapest
happy → happier → happiest

Mit ***more*** und ***most*** werden gesteigert:
- zwei- und mehrsilbige Adjektive,
- Adjektive, die auf *-ing* enden.

famous → more famous → most famous
boring → more boring → most boring

Achtung: Bei der Steigerung verändert sich oft die Schreibweise der Adjektive:
- Der Endkonsonant wird verdoppelt.
- Ein *-y* am Schluss wird durch *-i* ersetzt.
- Das stumme *-e* fällt weg.

hot → hotter → hottest
big → bigger → biggest
funny → funnier → funniest
angry → angrier → angriest
nice → nicer → nicest
close → closer → closest

Vergleicht man verschiedene Dinge oder Menschen, steht:
- Komparativ + ***than*** (Steigerung),
- ***(not) as*** + Adjektiv + ***as*** (Vergleich)

Ernie is **older than** (älter als) Ben.
This is **more important than** (wichtiger als) that.
This book is **as** cheap **as** (so billig wie) that CD.
Tina is not **as** intelligent **as** (nicht so intelligent wie) Peter.

ÜBUNG 1 **Unterstreiche alle Adjektive, die sich hier verbergen.**

nice – traffic – terrible – to walk – finger – happy – knee – wives – short – shelves – expensive – to laugh – dream – to hear – soft – hard – to find – tree – feeling – cheap – church – flower – to smell – tall – big – behind – after – to feel – rich

ÜBUNG 2 **Suche jeweils ein passendes Adjektiv zu einem Substantiv (Nomen). Schreibe die Lösungen, mit einem unbestimmten Artikel, in dein Übungsheft.**

tall – high – small – red – bad – exciting – long – funny

woman – train – mountain – car – tomato – computer game – joke – dream

ÜBUNG 3 **Stelle Vergleiche an. Schreibe jeweils zwei Sätze.**

fast: plane – train

Planes are faster than trains. Trains are not as fast as planes.

high: Zugspitze – Mount Everest

small: mouse – elephant

old: my granddad – my mum

difficult: maths – biology

expensive: computer – mobile phone

nice: my English teacher – my maths teacher

WISSEN +

Unregelmäßig gesteigerte Adjektive
Unregelmäßige Formen haben:
gut: ***good*** *→ better → best*
schlecht: ***bad*** *→ worse → worst*

weit entfernt: ***far*** *→ farther / further → farthest / furthest*

My bike is better than yours.
Today the weather is worse than yesterday.
London is farther away from New York than from Paris.

Mit *-er / -est* statt mit *more / most* werden diese zweisilbigen Adjektive gesteigert:
klug: ***clever*** *→ cleverer → cleverest*
ruhig: ***quiet*** *→ quieter → quietest*
eng: ***narrow*** *→ narrower → narrowest*

Randy is cleverer than we are, isn't he? – Yes, he is the cleverest boy in class.
Be careful! The road is narrower than I thought.

ÜBUNG 4 **Hier darfst du mal richtig angeben. Steigere die Adjektive.**

a friend:	**you:**
My dad is rich.	My dad is richer. He's the richest person in the world.
My sister is beautiful.	My sister ______ ______ girl in the world.
I'm clever.	I'm ______ ______ boy / girl in class.
My bike is fast.	My ______ ______ bike in town.
I'm happy.	I'm ______ ______ person on earth.
This film is good.	That ______ ______ film ever.
My dog is really lazy.	My dog ______ ______ dog in the world.
My brother is tall.	My brother ______ ______ in our family.

WISSEN

Die Stellung der Adjektive **Attributiver** Gebrauch: Wenn ein **Adjektiv** ein Substantiv näher beschreibt, steht es direkt **vor** dem Substantiv.	The **little** cat is sitting on the **old** tree.
Prädikativer Gebrauch: Das **Adjektiv** steht **nach** to be und **nach** den Verben *to feel – sich fühlen, to look – aussehen,* *to sound – sich anhören, to smell – riechen,* *to taste – schmecken,* wenn sie als Zustandsverben gebraucht werden.	The girl is **nice.** He feels **happy.** She looks **sad.** The chips *(Pommes frites)* taste **good.**

ÜBUNG 5 **Bilde aus den folgenden Wörtern Sätze. Trage die Sätze in der richtigen Spalte ein und unterstreiche das Adjektiv.**

chocolate / to like / the lady / young
big / the table / to be
to feel / my friends / happy
Tim / sad / to look
she / to love / her ring / new
cool / sunglasses / wearing / they're

attributiver Gebrauch	prädikativer Gebrauch
The young lady likes chocolate.	

ÜBUNG 6 **Übersetze den folgenden Text. Schreibe in dein Übungsheft.**

Tina ist groß, aber Jenny ist größer. Jenny ist so groß wie Ben.
Sei vorsichtig! Du musst vorsichtiger sein als gestern.
Im April ist das Wetter schlecht, aber im November ist es schlechter.
Am schlechtesten ist es im Januar.
Ich bin so klug wie … *(Such dir jemanden aus!).*

ÜBEN

1.2 Adverbien der Art und Weise

Adverbien *(adverbs)* beschreiben eine Tätigkeit näher. Mit ihnen gibst du an, *wie* oder *auf welche Weise* man etwas macht.	He walks **slowly.** (*Wie* läuft er? Er läuft langsam.)
Adverbien bestimmen also ein Verb näher. Sie können jedoch auch ein Adjektiv genauer beschreiben.	Tim **works carefully.** (Das Verb wird näher bestimmt.) The book was **terribly boring.** (Das Adjektiv wird näher bestimmt.)
Das Adverb wird gebildet, indem man die Endung *-ly* an das Adjektiv hängt.	quiet → quietly nice → nicely
Aufgepasst: Einige Besonderheiten musst du beachten: ■ Endet das Adjektiv auf *-y*, wird die Adverbendung zu *-ily*. ■ Endet das Adjektiv auf *-le*, lautet die Adverbendung *-ly*. ■ Endet das Adjektiv auf *-ic*, ist die Adverbendung *-ically*.	happy → happily easy → easily simple → simply terrible → terribly basic → basically

Die Steigerung von Adverbien

Die meisten Adverbien auf *-ly* werden mit ***more*** und ***most*** gesteigert.	I write more carefully than my brother. But my mother writes most carefully.
Merke: Auch hier gibt es unregelmäßige Bildungen: *good (gut):* Adverb *well* → *better* → *best*	I can speak English very well, better than French.
bad (schlecht): Adverb *badly* → *worse* → *worst*	I slept badly last night, worse than last week.
Der Vergleich von Adverbien erfolgt wie bei den Adjektiven: ■ *(not) as* ... Adverb + *as* (Vergleich)	I work **as** carefully **as** Simon. Ron doesn't work **as** carefully **as** Kim.
■ Komparativ oder Superlativ des Adverbs + *than*	Lizzy does her homework **more carefully than** her sister.

ÜBUNG 7 **Unterstreiche in den Sätzen das Adverb.**

My grandmother speaks quietly.

The pupils laughed loudly.

You can guess the answer easily.

She walked slowly out of the room.

Manchester United played badly and lost the match.

ÜBUNG 8 **Bilde die Adverbform der Adjektive im Wortspeicher.**

loud – quiet – good – happy – careful – nervous – nice – lucky

ÜBUNG 9 **Welches Adverb passt zu welchem Verb? Bilde jeweils einen einfachen Satz und schreibe die Sätze in dein Übungsheft.**

Beispiel: Brad – write – carefully → Brad writes carefully.

Mark – Simon – they – Peggy – I

shout – smile – drink – speak English – play soccer

angrily – happily – quickly – well – badly

WISSEN

Verschiedene Arten von Adverbien
Neben den Adverbien der Art und Weise kennst du bereits weitere Adverbarten:

- Adverbien der Zeit: *Wann* passiert etwas? — I'm coming home **today.**
- Adverbien des Ortes: *Wo* passiert etwas? — John is **outside.**
- Häufigkeitsadverbien: *Wie oft* geschieht etwas? (Stellung im Satz: ↑ S. 12) — I **often** go shopping with my mum.
- Gradadverbien: Sie verstärken eine Aussage oder schwächen sie ab. — There was a lot of snow. I **almost** fell and broke my leg.
- Satzadverbien: Sie beziehen sich auf den ganzen Satz. — **Of course** I know the answer.

ÜBUNG 10 **Finde die acht Adverbien in dem Wortgitter. Achtung: Es verstecken sich auch ein Häufigkeitsadverb und ein Adverb der Zeit darin!**

A	L	N	P	W	E	X	T	R	E	M	E	L	Y	V	I	Q	A	R
E	E	S	X	Z	J	P	L	K	O	T	G	C	S	D	Y	S	J	Z
B	A	G	J	Y	I	V	A	T	U	R	D	H	Z	R	T	A	B	X
F	S	K	W	M	O	X	Q	M	Y	H	S	F	C	D	O	C	X	W
H	I	L	E	N	G	R	H	A	P	P	I	L	Y	U	D	Z	L	B
M	L	R	L	F	B	F	E	E	G	E	T	C	D	K	A	M	B	L
T	Y	O	L	F	W	U	C	I	R	Q	B	A	D	L	Y	J	M	I
N	Q	E	H	P	V	P	J	N	S	E	P	B	D	U	V	N	O	Z
M	U	I	O	F	T	E	N	H	K	Q	H	F	X	O	W	C	G	A
L	A	D	K	K	T	J	I	O	C	A	R	E	F	U	L	L	Y	Y

ÜBUNG 11 **Ergänze die Tabelle mit den richtigen Adverbformen.**

to watch	carefully	more carefully	most carefully
to cycle	well		
to speak		more clearly	
to write		worse	
to speak	slowly		
to play volleyball			best
to talk		more loudly	

ÜBUNG 12 **Wandle die Aussagen in Sätze mit Adverbien um. Das Verb des Satzes kannst du in der Regel aus der Personenbezeichnung ableiten.**

Beispiel: James is a careful driver. → James drives carefully.

Betty is a perfect tennis player.
John is a nervous speaker.
They are careful readers.

Christy is a good dancer.
The rain is heavy in October.
My father is a fantastic cook.

ÜBUNG 13 **Höre dir Track 1 auf der CD an und setze das passende Adverb ein. Achte auf Steigerungs- und Vergleichsformen!**

1

Dear Peter,

How are you? I hope you are doing as ______ as I am. Let me tell you about a great day. Yesterday, I went to a birthday party. At the beginning I stood ______ alone because I didn't know anybody. But then some boys and girls came over and talked to me. We played badminton in the garden. I played ______ but the others played much ______. I was on a good team, so we won the match ______. When it got dark, we made a bonfire (Lagerfeuer) ______. One of the boys played the guitar. We sang "Happy Birthday" ______ and started dancing ______. It was so much fun. But the best part of the evening was the fireworks at the end. Everyone watched ______ (aufgeregt).

Write back soon!

Yours, Mark

WISSEN

Die Stellung der Adverbien
Adverbien der Art und Weise stehen meist am Satzende.
Häufigkeitsadverbien stehen vor dem Verb.

Jeff opens the bag **slowly.**
Sandy listened to her mum **nervously.**
I **often** go skiing with my friends.
Sue **usually** tidies her room on Sundays.

ÜBUNG 14 **Übersetze. Schreibe die Sätze in dein Übungsheft.**

Ich gehe oft ins Kino.
Ich spreche gut Englisch.
Martin steht normalerweise um 7 Uhr auf.
Basketball spiele ich schlecht.

ÜBEN

1.3 Adjektive und Adverbien im Vergleich

Adjektive und Adverbien bestimmen einen Satzteil (meist Substantiv und Verb) näher. Durch sie kannst du etwas genauer beschreiben.

It's summer and the sun is shining.
→ It's a very **hot** summer and the sun is shining **brightly.**

Adjektive beziehen sich auf Substantive oder Pronomen. Sie beschreiben, wie jemand oder etwas ist.

Sam is happy. He's a happy boy.
The mountain is high. It's a high mountain.

Adverbien beziehen sich auf Verben oder Adjektive. Sie beschreiben, wie etwas getan wird oder wie sich etwas verhält.

Sam sings happily.
The book is terribly exciting.

Merke:
- Nach einem Zustandsverb (↑ S. 8) steht ein Adjektiv!
- Nach einem Tätigkeitsverb steht ein Adverb!

Ron looks angry. → verärgert aussehen: ein Zustand
Ron looks angrily at his teacher.
→ verärgert schauen: eine Tätigkeit

Besonderheiten bei der Adverbbildung

Es gibt eine Reihe von Adverbien, die die Form von Adjektiven haben:

early – früh	*late – spät*
fast – schnell	*long – lange*
high – hoch	*low – niedrig*

Susie is fast (Adjektiv). Susie runs fast (Adverb).
I get up early and I go to bed late.
Don't climb so high, it's dangerous.

Aufgepasst: Von einigen Adjektiven gibt es zwei Adverbformen, die unterschiedliche Bedeutung haben!

hard (hart)	↔	*hardly (kaum)*
pretty (ziemlich)	↔	*prettily (hübsch, schön)*
near (nahe)	↔	*nearly (fast)*

Linda works hard. She hardly sleeps.
Anna isn't only pretty clever, she also dresses prettily.
Ben drove too near the river. He nearly had an accident.

Merke: Well kann nicht nur das Adverb von *good* sein, sondern auch ein eigenständiges Adjektiv! Es bedeutet dann *gesund.*

Ralph is ill. But he sleeps well (schläft gut), and soon he will be well (gesund) again.

ÜBUNG 15 **Hier kannst du den Unterschied zwischen einem Satz mit Adjektiv und einem Satz mit Adverb gut erkennen. Setze das fehlende Wort ein.**

happy	adjective:	Sam is happy.
	adverb:	Sam sings happily.
slow	adjective:	A VW Beetle is a ______ car.
	adverb:	A VW Beetle driver drives ______.
sad	adjective:	It's a ______ story.
	adverb:	He tells the story ______.
nervous	adjective:	Tim is very ______.
	adverb:	He talks ______.
quiet	adjective:	Lisa is a ______ girl.
	adverb:	She talks ______.

ÜBUNG 16 **Überlege, welche Adjektive und Adverbien hier passen könnten.**

This is a ______ car. It drives ______.
He's a ______ boy. He works ______.
The basketball match is ______. The players play ______.

ÜBUNG 17 **Setze die richtige Form ein. Handelt es sich um ein Adjektiv oder ein Adverb?**

A cheetah *(Gepard)* is a ______ (schnell) animal. A panther runs ______ (schnell), too.
Richard is a ______ (hart) worker. Susan works ______ (hart), too. But Tim ______ (kaum) works at all.
Anne is a ______ (hübsch) girl. She talks ______ (ziemlich) cool. And she laughs ______ (schön).
Marc is a ______ (gut) player. And Kim plays ______ (gut), too.
How do you feel today? – I'm ______ (gesund) again, thank you.

ÜBEN

ÜBUNG 18 **Zustands- oder Tätigkeitsverb? Entscheide, ob du ein Adjektiv oder ein Adverb einsetzen musst.**

The soup smells __________ (gut).

David has got a cold. He can't smell __________ (gut).

The fish tastes __________ (schlecht).

Marc tastes the meal __________ (vorsichtig).

George looks at his brother __________ (ärgerlich).

Linda isn't happy at all *(überhaupt nicht)*.

She looks very __________ (ärgerlich).

ÜBUNG 19 **Ersetze in den folgenden Sätzen die rot markierten Wörter duch die richtigen englischen Adjektiv- oder Adverbformen und schreibe die Sätze in dein Übungsheft.**

My brother is (größer als) my sister.
The (alt) lady looks (ziemlich) (unglücklich).
It was the (schlimmster) day of my life: Someone stole my (neu) bike and I had a (schrecklich) toothache.
Computer games are (nicht so interessant wie) going on a (gefährlich) trip.
It was night. Teresa (kaum) saw anything.

ÜBUNG 20 **Übersetze.**

Ich stehe jeden Tag früh auf.

____

Mein Vater fährt schneller als meine Mutter.

____

Rita sieht traurig aus. Sie fühlt sich schlecht.

____

Du sprichst gut Englisch.

____

Klassenarbeit 1

45 Minuten

AUFGABE 1 Finde das passende Adjektiv und die dazugehörigen Steigerungsformen.

	Positiv	Komparativ	Superlativ
groß			
glücklich			
gefährlich			
gut			
schlecht			

AUFGABE 2 Setze die Adjektive ein und verwandle sie in Adverbien.

	Adjektiv	Adverb		Adjektiv	Adverb
vorsichtig			einfach		
furchtbar			fantastisch		
früh			schnell		

AUFGABE 3 Lies den Text durch und unterstreiche Adjektive blau und Adverbien rot.

Great fun and better marks

Do you want to improve *(verbessern)* your English quickly and make new friends around the world? If yes, then join our interesting exchange programme *(Austauschprogramm)* and spend your holiday in beautiful Great Britain!

You live comfortably with nice families. In the morning you'll study English in groups with friendly teachers. In the afternoons we'll take you on exciting trips. You'll visit important sights, take part in different sports activities, and meet new friends quickly. Isn't this the perfect way to learn English? If you are interested, please contact "Fun-Tours".

TESTEN

AUFGABE 4 **Entscheide dich: Adjektiv oder Adverb?**

Dear Jennifer Lopez,

My name is Gina and I am a ______ (big) fan of yours. I think you are very ______ (pretty) and that you dance ______ (beautiful). I would like to dance as ______ (good) as you. Last year I started dancing lessons. The instructor (Lehrer) is very ______ (strict) but I am getting ______ (good) ______ (quick).

My ______ (secret) wish is to dance ______ (professional) in one of your shows. How did you start your ______ (wonderful) career? Please give me some ______ (helpful) advice (Rat).

Your fan Gina

AUFGABE 5 **Übersetze die Sätze. Achte auf die Satzstellung und alle Besonderheiten!**

Richard öffnet seine Tasche langsam.

Mein Vater ist ein vorsichtiger Fahrer.

Es ist ein schneller Zug. Er fährt *(to travel)* sehr schnell.

Betty ist ziemlich klug.

Harry arbeitet sehr hart. Er schläft kaum.

Jim tanzt sehr gut. Er ist ein guter Tänzer.

Klassenarbeit 2

60 Minuten

AUFGABE 6 **Steigerung bei Adjektiven und Adverbien: Setze die fehlenden Formen ein.**

good		
		most carefully
	worse	
		most terribly
	easier	
		greatest
slowly		
	narrower	
expensive		

AUFGABE 7 **Setze die passende Form ein. Achte auf eventuelle Steigerungsformen!**

Jenny feels ________ (besser als) yesterday but not ________ (gut) enough to go to school.

Sarah looked around ________ (nervös) and started to speak ________ (leise).

Jenny's mother opened the letter ________ (vorsichtig). It was a ________ (lang) letter with ________ (wunderschön) handwriting.

Mum drives ________ (schneller als) dad. She is not ________ (so vorsichtig wie) he is.

The police did a ________ (gut) job. They did their job very ________ (gut).

TESTEN

AUFGABE 8 **Schreibe vollständige Sätze. Achte darauf, dass das Adjektiv an der richtigen Stelle im Satz steht.**

Mr Smith / teacher / old

Los Angeles / city / famous

Brad Pitt / actor / good-looking

Ants / animals / small

AUFGABE 9 **Setze die angegebenen Adjektive in der richtigen Steigerungsform in die Lücke. Aufgepasst: Bei zwei Sätzen musst du den Superlativ verwenden.**

Angelina Jolie is ______ (pretty) than our teacher.

My mum is ______ (young) than my friend's mum.

Mr Bond is ______ (handsome) than our neighbour.

The A 380 Airbus is ______ (big) airplane in the world.

My Dad is ______ (strong) than me.

Our school is ______ (ugly) building in town.

A cat is ______ (intelligent) than a fish.

AUFGABE 10 **Ordne die im Wortspeicher angegebenen Adverbien richtig zu.**

there – slowly – today – lately – carefully – here – everywhere – already – happily – simply – outside – tomorrow – basically – badly

Art und Weise	Zeit	Ort

AUFGABE 11 **Adjektiv oder Adverb? Ergänze die Sätze.**

It is not ______ (easy) to write a book.

Please remember to ride your bike ______ (careful). You often drive too ______ (quick).

My mum is very ______ (unhappy) because I don't write my homework ______ (tidy).

Dennis feels ______ (nervous) because he has a dentist's appointment in the afternoon.

The bus arrived ______ (late) again and so I missed the beginning of the show.

Pupils often think that they work ______ (hard) than their teachers.

AUFGABE 12 **Schreibe ganze Sätze. Achte darauf, die Adverbien an der richtigen Stelle im Satz zu platzieren (Ort vor Zeit!) und die richtige Zeit zu verwenden.**

Peter / outside / to go / yesterday

______

Mr Smith / at the office / to arrive / at 8:30 a.m. / every weekday

______

You / to stop smoking / definitely / should

______

He / a lot / last week / to eat and to drink

______

AUFGABE 13 **Übersetze. Schreibe in dein Übungsheft.**

Mein Vater spricht sehr schlecht Englisch.
Lilly spielt gut Cello.
Sie sangen das Geburtstagslied laut.
Sie wartete aufgeregt auf ihren Freund.
Das Essen riecht gut.
Mutter sieht ziemlich ärgerlich aus.

2

Modale Hilfsverben

2.1 Das Hilfsverb *können*

Die modalen Hilfsverben *can (können)* und *could* (Form im *simple past*) (↑ Kap. 3.2) stehen immer mit einem Vollverb.	Gina **can ride** a horse. We **could go** to the cinema. **Can you** ride a horse?
Mit *can* und *could* können auch Verneinungen und Fragen gebildet werden.	You **can't go** out now. **Couldn't** you **come** earlier?
Aufgepasst: Can darf im Gegensatz zum Deutschen niemals allein stehen!	Ich kann Englisch. → I can speak English.
Das Hilfsverb ***can*** drückt aus: ■ eine Fähigkeit oder Unfähigkeit, ■ eine Erlaubnis oder ein Verbot, ■ eine Bitte, ■ eine Möglichkeit oder Unmöglichkeit.	 I can speak French. / I can't help you. You can park here. / You can't park here. Can I get your pen? That can't be Mrs Cooper.
Das Hilfsverb ***could*** bezeichnet ■ die Vergangenheitsform *(konnte)*, ■ eine höfliche Frage *(könnte)*.	 My grandfather could speak Greek. Could you pass me the sugar, please?
Aufgepasst: Can und *could* sind nur im *simple present* und im *simple past* verwendbar. Für alle anderen Zeiten brauchst du die **Ersatzform** ***to be able to*** *(können, fähig sein)*. *Merke: Can/could* bezeichnet eine allgemeine Fähigkeit, *to be able to* bezieht sich auf eine spezielle Situation.	 *simple present:* I can ride a bike. *simple past:* He could not find his pen. *will-future:* He won't be able to repair his car. I can swim very fast. I am able to break the school record.
Die verneinten Formen lauten: *can* → *cannot* (Kurzform *can't*) *could* → *could not* (Kurzform *couldn't*) *to be able to* → *to be not able to*	 I can't open the door. He couldn't do his homework. He wasn't able to open the door.

ÜBUNG 1 **Was kannst du, was nicht? Was ist erlaubt, was nicht? Schreibe in dein Übungsheft.**

Beispiel: to play / the guitar / the trumpet → I can play the guitar. I cannot / can't play the trumpet.

to ride / a horse / an elephant
to speak / English / Chinese
to repair / a bike / a car
to go / to Italy / to the moon
to drink lemonade / beer

ÜBUNG 2 **Setze *can, cannot, could* oder *could not* ein.**

_____ you give me the book, please?

Thomas and Tina _____ do a lot of tricks.

When I was young I _____ walk on my hands.

I _____ do it now.

You can take my old bike. But you _____ use my new bike.

King Edward I lived from 1239 – 1307. He _____ speak different languages. But he _____ use a computer. They had no computers around 1300.

ÜBUNG 3 **Setze die passende Form des englischen Hilfsverbs *können* in die Lücke. Manchmal gibt es zwei Möglichkeiten – trage beide ein. Achte auf die Zeiten!**

Last year we _____ go to India.

At the moment Marc _____ (not) play the guitar. But he has got a teacher now. Next year he _____ *(will-future)* play the guitar.

Toby _____ (not) ride a bike when he was three.

But now he's twelve, so he _____ ride a bike.

_____ to climb Mount Everest?

ÜBEN

2.2 Das Hilfsverb *dürfen*

Wenn man eine Erlaubnis ausdrücken möchte, muss man in allen Zeiten – außer im *simple present* – die **Ersatzform** ***to be allowed to*** *(dürfen)* verwenden.	*simple present:* Jane can / is allowed to come. *simple past:* She was allowed to come. *will-future:* She will be allowed to come.
Die **Verneinung** wird mit *not* gebildet und drückt ein Verbot aus: *to be not allowed to (nicht dürfen)*	Jane is not allowed to go to Peter's party tonight. She wasn't allowed to come. She won't be allowed to come.
Wenn man eine höfliche Frage stellen will, verwendet man statt *can* das Hilfsverb ***may***.	May we (könnten / dürften wir) have a cup of tea, please? May I go to the concert?
May kann auch ein Verbot oder eine Erlaubnis ausdrücken. Es ist formeller als *can*.	Tourists may use the swimming pool from 9 a.m. till 5 p.m. Guests may not smoke. Visitors may not walk on the grass in public gardens.
Das Hilfsverb *may* wird auch verwendet, um eine Vermutung auszudrücken.	He might be sick. Jane might buy a new dress für Linda's party.
Neben der allgemeinen Verneinungsform *to be not allowed to* wird eine weitere Form der Verneinung mit ***mustn't*** gebildet. Sie bezeichnet ein strenges Verbot (↑ Kap. 2.3).	Ben mustn't watch (darf nicht) TV in the evenings. You mustn't steal your brother's toys! You mustn't drive a car! You haven't got a licence *(Führerschein)*.

ÜBUNG 4 **Verwende *(not) to be allowed to*. Schreibe die Sätze in dein Übungsheft.**

to go swimming	✓	to watch the show	✗
to run fast	✗	to do the washing-up	✓
to sing a love song	✓	to watch a film on TV	✓
to play a computer game	✗	to go to the party	✗

WISSEN

Modale Hilfsverben wie *can, could, may, must* stehen immer mit einem Vollverb (ohne *to*). *Merke:* Sie haben in der 3. Person Singular Präsens kein *-s*.	I can hear music. You may use the bathroom. I must get up. He can help me.
Primäre Hilfsverben sind *to be, to have, to do*. Wie die modalen Hilfsverben bilden auch sie Fragen, Verneinungen und Zeiten.	He is cleaning the window. Kim hasn't been here for two years. Did you like the concert?

ÜBUNG 5 **Höre dir Track 2 auf der CD an und setze die fehlenden Formen ein. Achte auch auf Signalwörter, die dir Hinweise auf die richtige Zeitform geben.**

2

You ________ turn left (Verbot), but you ________ (Erlaubnis) turn right.

________ (höfliche Frage) I help you with your work?

She ________ (Verbot) borrow *(leihen)* the skateboard last week.

________ (you, Erlaubnis) watch TV last week?

Dogs ________ in the cinema (Verbot).

You ________ (starkes Verbot) bring your dog.

Visitors ________ (höflich formuliertes Verbot) use their mobile phones during the show.

ÜBUNG 6 **Übersetze die folgenden Sätze. Schreibe in dein Übungsheft.**

Jane durfte uns besuchen.
Tom wird nicht bleiben dürfen.
Darf er mit uns kommen?

2.3 Das Hilfsverb *müssen*

Das Hilfsverb ***must*** bezeichnet ■ eine Notwendigkeit und Verpflichtung, ■ eine Gewissheit, ■ eine Schlussfolgerung oder ■ eine Aufforderung.	 I must go now. Tim must be tired. He stayed up long. It's 2 o'clock now. School must be over. You must be quiet now.
Must wird mit ***need not*** (Kurzform ***needn't***) oder ***do not have to*** (Kurzform ***don't have to***) verneint.	I must go to school, but I needn't go/don't have to go to the sports club.
Must und *needn't* kannst du nur in der Gegenwart verwenden. Für die anderen Zeiten brauchst du die **Ersatzform** ***to have to / to have got to*** – müssen	I must tidy my room today. → I had to tidy my room yesterday. You needn't do your homework. → You will not (won't) have to do your homework tomorrow.
Aufgepasst: Bildest du eine **Verneinung** oder eine **Frage** mit der Ersatzform *to have got to*, musst du das Hilfsverb *to do* verwenden. Das *got* entfällt. Im *simple past* nimmst du statt *do* die Form *did*.	Do you have to get up early? No, I don't have to get up early. Did she have to work last week? – No, she didn't have to work last week.
Achtung: Zwischen *must* und *to have to* gibt es einen Bedeutungsunterschied: ■ *must* drückt ein **persönliches Bedürfnis** aus, ■ *to have to* bezeichnet einen **äußeren Zwang**.	 I am hungry. I must eat something. I have to go shopping. My mother told me to.
Merke: must heißt *müssen*, *mustn't* heißt *nicht dürfen*!	You must tell the truth. You mustn't eat all the cookies.

WISSEN

ÜBUNG 7 **Pits Mutter sagt Pit, was er alles zu tun hat. Setze in den gelben Feldern *must* und das passende Verb ein.**

Mum: "Pit, after school you ______ your bike! Then you ______. You ______ it to your father in the evening. At 5 o'clock you ______. And at 9 o'clock you ______. You ______ early tomorrow!"

ÜBUNG 8 **Am nächsten Tag erzählt Pit seinen Freunden, was er gestern alles tun musste. Schreibe den Text aus Übung 7 in dein Übungsheft. Setze das *simple past* von *to have to* ein. Achtung: Statt *you/your* brauchst du nun *I/my*!**
Beginne folgendermaßen: Pit: "After school I had to clean my bike."

ÜBUNG 9 **Achte auf den Bedeutungsunterschied: *must* (persönliches Bedürfnis) oder *to have to* (äußerer Zwang)?**

My teacher is very strict *(streng)*. I ______ do my homework.
I have been running for one hour. I ______ drink something.
Mother to Jill: "Don't be late! You ______ be home at 10 o'clock!" – Jill to her friends: "I ______ be home at 10. My mother told me so."

ÜBEN

WISSEN +

Fragen und Verneinungen
Fragen und Verneinungen werden bei den modalen Hilfsverben direkt mit dem Hilfsverb gebildet – nicht mit *to do* (außer bei *to have to*). Beachte die Wortstellung in den Beispielen.

Can I help you? – No, you cannot help me.
May I turn the light off? – No, you may not turn the light off.
Were you able to find it? – No, we were not able to find it.
Am I allowed to come in? – No, you are not allowed to come in.

ÜBUNG 10 **Bilde die richtigen Fragen und Verneinungen.**

to be allowed to – you / go *(simple past)*:

Were you allowed to go to the party? –

No, I wasn't allowed to go to the party.

can – we / help *(simple present)*:

______ you, sir? –

No, you ______.

to be allowed to – he / take *(simple present)*:

______ this bike? –

No, he ______.

may – I / have:

______ a bottle of coke, please? –

No, you ______.

to be allowed to – she / call *(will-future)*:

______ me tomorrow? –

No, she ______ tomorrow.

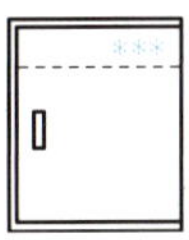

to be able to – we / repair *(simple past)*:

______ the fridge? –

No, we ______.

Can – you / see *(simple present)*:

______ the moon? – No, I ______.

WISSEN

Achtung Verwechslungsgefahr!
Don't have to, needn't und *mustn't* sind leicht zu verwechseln. Präge dir den Unterschied ein:
nicht müssen – don't have to
nicht brauchen – needn't
nicht dürfen – mustn't

Du **musst** das **nicht** tun. – You **don't have to** do that.
Du **brauchst** das **nicht** zu tun. – You **needn't** do that.
Du **darfst** das **nicht** tun. – You **mustn't** do that.

ÜBUNG 11 **Fülle die Lücken mit der passenden Form von *to have to*. Achte auf die Signalwörter für die Vergangenheit und für das *will-future*. Achtung: An zwei Stellen musst du eine Frage formulieren!**

A three-day snowboard course

Instructor: "Good morning everyone. How do you feel after your first day of snowboarding?"

Betty: "I feel good today but I ______ go to bed early yesterday. I was so tired."

Instructor: "That's alright. On your first day you ______ learn all the basics (*Grundlagen*). Today we will practise *(üben)* a lot. Remember, tomorrow you ______ pass a test. So we ______ start right away *(sofort)*."

John: "Can we put on our snowboards right now? Or ______ have a warming-up first?"

Instructor: "Of course, you always ______ do a warming-up first. Today you ______ get up the hill with the lift. To use the lift – what ______ do?"

Steven: "We ______ stand on the snowboard with one foot only."

Instructor: "You're right. Good luck – I will see you on top of the hill."

ÜBUNG 12 **Überlege, ob du *mustn't, needn't* oder *don't have to* einsetzen musst. Übersetze nur die roten Satzteile.**

Du musst nicht in die Schule gehen.

Du brauchst mir nicht zu helfen, ich komme allein zurecht.

Du darfst nicht zu viel trinken, du bekommst sonst Bauchweh.

Ihr braucht nicht zu bezahlen, ich lade euch ein.

Du musst heute nicht früh ins Bett gehen.

Ich darf heute nicht lange aufbleiben *(stay up)*.

ÜBUNG 13 **Im Englischunterricht kann man die modalen Hilfsverben gut verwenden. Wie lauten die richtigen Sätze? Höre dir dazu Track 3 auf der CD an. (Hinweis: Bei einigen Sätzen gibt es zwei Möglichkeiten.)**

3

Du bittest deinen Lehrer, etwas zu wiederholen *(repeat)*: "Can you repeat it, please?"

Du musst jetzt gehen: "I now."

Dein Lehrer braucht dir nicht helfen: "You ."

Ist es möglich, das Fenster zu öffnen: " the window?"

Du konntest gestern keine Hausaufgaben machen: "I yesterday."

Du möchtest eine Frage stellen: " ?"

Der Lehrer sagt, dass ihr leise sein müsst: "You ."

Klassenarbeit 1

45 Minuten

AUFGABE 1 **Verbinde die einzelnen Sätze mit der passenden Bedeutung durch eine Linie.**

May I have a glass of water, please?	Fähigkeit
The bus mustn't stop here.	Möglichkeit
You can do your homework later.	striktes Verbot
You must be careful.	Erlaubnis
Willy was able to dance.	höfliche Bitte
Are we allowed to listen?	Aufforderung

AUFGABE 2 **Bilde entsprechende Sätze im *simple present* und der 2. Person Singular (du). Achtung: Manchmal gibt es zwei Möglichkeiten!**

nicht dürfen: to sit here

You

müssen: to wear a helmet *(Helm)*

You

höfliche Bitte: to help you

You

nicht müssen: to wait for me

You

nicht brauchen: to do the washing-up

You

dürfen: to watch the film

You

können: to speak Chinese (Frage!)

AUFGABE 3 **Fit in allen Zeiten? Setze die Sätze in die angegebene Zeitform. Achte darauf, immer die Ersatzformen zu verwenden, und schreibe ganze Sätze.**

1. Tom can ride a motor bike.

   simple past:

   will-future:

2. She must write a story.

   simple past:

   will-future:

3. I can go camping with my friends. (Erlaubnis!)

   simple past:

   will-future:

4. Richard and Diana needn't come.

   simple past:

   will-future:

AUFGABE 4 **Übersetze die rot markierten Satzteile. Schreibe in dein Übungsheft.**

Ich durfte leider nicht fernsehen.
Musstet ihr gestern lange warten?
Wir konnten die Flasche nicht öffnen.
Wirst du morgen bei der Aufführung singen können?

AUFGABE 5 **Bilde Fragen und Verneinungen. Achte dabei auf die Zeiten! Schreibe die Sätze in dein Übungsheft.**

Musstet ihr gestern arbeiten?
Wirst du morgen kommen können?
Laila braucht nicht ins Bett zu gehen.
Darf ich dir eine Frage stellen?
Durfte Dean zuhören?
Vera darf nicht kommen.
Muss sie Tee trinken?

Klassenarbeit 2

45 Minuten

AUFGABE 6 **Setze die Hilfsverben *can, must* und *may* in der angegebenen Person in die richtige Form. Nenne, wo es möglich ist, immer auch die Ersatzformen.**

can → 1. Person Singular *simple present*

can → 3. Person Plural *simple past*

may → 2. Person Singular *future*

may → 1. Person Plural *simple past*

must → 1. Person Singular *simple past*

must → 2. Person Plural *future*

AUFGABE 7 **Wer kann was? Schreibe vollständige Sätze in dein Übungsheft.**

Beispiel: Mary / play the violin / swim → Mary can play the violin and can swim, but she can't ride a unicycle or do karate.

	play the violin	**ride a unicycle (Einrad)**	**swim**	**do karate**
Mary	✓	–	✓	–
Peter	–	–	✓	✓
Jamie	✓	✓	✓	–
Helena	–	✓	✓	–
Vicky	–	–	–	✓
Robin	–	–	✓	–

TESTEN

AUFGABE 8 ***To have to, to be allowed to, to be able to*? Setze das richtige Hilfsverb in die Lücke.**

Do you want to see a movie tonight? I'd really like, but I can't. I ______ study for my math exam.

Did you go to school yesterday? No, I didn't. I was ill and ______ stay in bed. I ______ get up and watch TV.

I went shopping yesterday. I really ______ buy a new pair of jeans because I tore my favourite jeans in a bike accident.

My leg is broken. I ______ do any sports for four weeks.

Mother to her daughter: You ______ go to that party next weekend if you help me tidy up the kitchen.

May I smoke? No, you ______ smoke inside here. This is a non-smoking building.

I can't go out tonight. I ______ finish my essay.

AUFGABE 9 ***Must, mustn't, needn't*? Setze das richtige Hilfsverb in die Lücke.**

You ______ have a passport when you travel to the USA.

You ______ exchange Euro money when you travel to Slovakia.

You ______ be late for school.

You ______ smoke inside this building.

AUFGABE 10 **Übersetze. Schreibe in dein Übungsheft.**

Ich spreche Französisch. Kann ich Ihnen helfen?
Wir könnten ins Kino gehen.
Jane darf nicht auf Peters Party gehen.
Ich muss heute mein Zimmer aufräumen.
Ich musste gestern mein Zimmer aufräumen.
I habe wirklich Hunger. Ich muss jetzt etwas essen.
Vor Gericht *(in court)* musst du die Wahrheit sagen.

3 Vergangenheit

3.1 Das *simple past*

Im Englischen benutzt man für die abgeschlossene Vergangenheit das ***simple past***.	Last week Mr Harris **was** in hospital. I **had** an accident yesterday.
Verwende das *simple past*, wenn ■ eine Handlung zu einem bestimmten Zeitpunkt in der Vergangenheit liegt und abgeschlossen ist, ■ mehrere Handlungen in der Vergangenheit aufeinander folgten und nun abgeschlossen sind.	Ryan was ill last Monday (→ jetzt ist er wieder gesund). We had a party two weeks ago (→ sie ist längst vorüber). We went home, had dinner and drank a cup of coffee.
Bei folgenden **Signalwörtern** musst du immer das *simple past* verwenden: yesterday – gestern last week/month/year – letzte Woche/letzter Monat/letztes Jahr ... ago – vor ... *in + Jahreszahl – Jahreszahl*	I was at home **yesterday.** **Last summer** she met Susan. **Three years ago** we were in Spain. **In 2008** the Olympic Games were in Beijing.

Das *simple past* bei regelmäßigen Verben

Es gibt **regelmäßige** und **unregelmäßige** Verben. Das *simple past* von regelmäßigen Verben bildest du so: Grundform des Verbs (ohne *to*) + *-ed*	rain + -ed → rained talk + -ed → talked ask + -ed → asked
Achte hier auf die **Schreibung:** ■ Steht ein *-e* am Wortende, wird nur ein *-d* hinzugefügt, ■ Konsonant + *-y* wird zu *-ied*, ■ betonter Einzelvokal + Konsonant am Ende führen zur Konsonantenverdopplung.	to live → lived, to phone → phoned to try → tried, to worry → worried to stop → stopped, to spot → spotted

ÜBUNG 1 **Setze die richtige Verbform im *simple past* ein.**

Two thousand years ago,

people ______ (to live) differently.

They ______ (to own) no cars and

______ (to use) no mobile phones.

They ______ (to talk) about different

things and ______ (to like) different clothes.

ÜBUNG 2 **Schreibe alle *simple past*-Formen aus der Wortschlange in dein Übungsheft.**

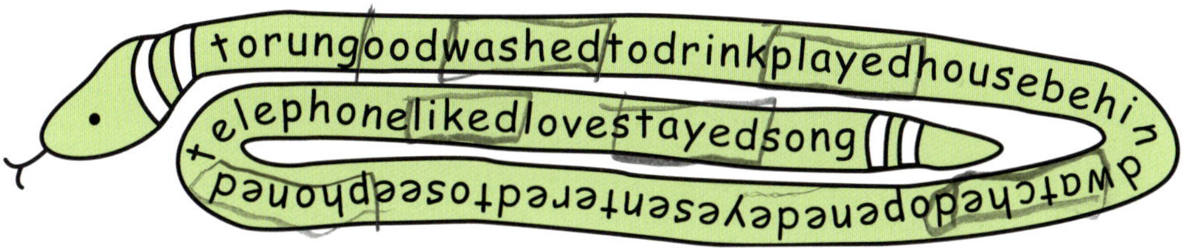

WISSEN

Aussprache

Aufgepasst: Die *simple past*-Formen werden verschieden ausgesprochen:

- Nach Vokal und stimmhaftem Konsonant folgt [d], — phoned [fəʊnd], stayed [steɪd]
- nach stimmlosem Konsonant folgt [t], — worked [wɜːkt], helped [helpt]
- nach [d] oder [t] folgt [ɪd]. — waited ['weɪtɪd], wanted ['wɒntɪd]

ÜBUNG 3 **Bilde die richtige *simple past*-Form. Bei Besonderheiten der Aussprache schreibe die Endung der *simple past*-Form in eckige Klammer.**

to phone →	phoned [d]	to want →	wanted [ɪd]
to worry →		to tidy →	
to work →		to arrive →	
to stop →		to live →	
to wait →		to like →	

ÜBEN

ÜBUNG 4 **Unterstreiche in dem folgenden Brief die *simple past*-Formen der regelmäßigen Verben.**

Dear Bill,
Last week I travelled from Germany to London with my class. We saw a lot of buildings and places, and on our last day we visited Madame Tussaud's, the wax figure museum. We looked at all the wax figures of famous (berühmt) people, for example the Queen, Madonna, and Michael Jackson. We had our cameras with us and had a lot of fun. When we entered another room, somebody shouted: "Elvis lives!" We turned around and could see the Elvis figure. We were very frightened because suddenly Elvis started to move and play the guitar. When the shock was over, we started to laugh: It was just a joke – we noticed that Elvis was just an actor.
Hope to hear from you soon!
Yours, Peter

ÜBUNG 5 **Trage nun alle regelmäßigen *simple past*-Formen in die Tabelle ein (ohne Dopplungen) und leite den passenden Infinitiv mit *to* ab.**

simple past	Grundform mit *to*	*simple past*	Grundform mit *to*

ÜBUNG 6 **Letztes Wochenende hatten Susan und Toby viel zu tun. Bilde Sätze im *simple past*. Schreibe sie in dein Übungsheft.**

Susan / to water / the flowers.
Toby / to tidy *(aufräumen)* / his room.
Susan and Toby / to clean / the kitchen.
Toby / to repair / his bike.
Susan / to play / with the dogs.
Susan / to work / with her father.
They / to watch / TV / in the evening.

3.2 Das *simple past* bei unregelmäßigen Verben

Für die Bildung des *simple past* bei unregelmäßigen Verben gibt es keine festen Regeln. Daher musst du dir die Formen genau einprägen und am besten auswendig lernen.	to do → did I did the washing-up. to write → wrote Ricky wrote a letter.
Eine Zusammenstellung der wichtigsten unregelmäßigen Verben findest du auf S. 52.	to get → got Tina got a letter.
Für die Bildung des *simple past* verwendet man die 2. Verbform.	to forget → forgot Tina forgot her brother's birthday.
Bei einigen Verben sind verschiedene *simple past*-Formen möglich, verwenden darfst du beide:	
to learn → learned / learnt (lernen)	Last year I learned to play tennis.
to dream → dreamed / dreamt (träumen)	Last night I dreamt of you.
Die *simple past*-Formen der wichtigsten **Modalverben** lauten: *can → could* *must → had to* *needn't → didn't have to*	 Last night I couldn't sleep. I had to do my homework before dinner. I didn't have to be home before dinner.
Bei einigen Verben wird die Verbform im *simple past* **nicht verändert**: *to cost → cost (kosten)* *to cut → cut (schneiden)* *to hit → hit (schlagen)* *to hurt → hurt (verletzen)* *to let → let (lassen)* *to put → put (setzen, stellen, legen)*	 The CDs cost (kosten / kosteten) twenty pounds. I cut (schneide / schnitt) the bread with a knife. I let (lasse / ließ) the dog out. They put (stellen / stellten) the books onto the shelf.
Achtung: Beim Verb *to read* ändert sich beim Übergang ins *simple past* zwar nicht die Schreibung, aber die Aussprache: to read [riːd] → read [red] (lesen)	 Tim read an interesting book last week.

Das *simple past* von *to be* und *to have*

Das unregelmäßige Verb ***to be*** hat im *simple past* die beiden Formen ***was*** und ***were:***

Singular:
I was — I was happy.
you were — Were you in school yesterday?
he/she/it was — She was lazy.

Plural:
we were — On Sunday we were in town.
you were — You were very brave, girls!
they were — They were happy

Das unregelmäßige Verb ***to have*** wird im *simple past* zu ***had.*** Es bleibt in allen Personalformen gleich.

I had a headache yesterday.
Last year she had short hair.
We had fun at the party.

Fragen und Verneinungen im *simple past*

Fragen in der Vergangenheit werden in der Regel mit *did* gebildet, der *simple past*-Form des unregelmäßigen Hilfsverbs *to do*.

Did you lose your keys?

Didn't she look great yesterday?

Bei **Verneinungen** benötigst du die verneinte Form von *did*, also *did not/didn't*, sowie die Grundform des Vollverbs.

Tom sold his bike, but he did not/didn't sell his game boy.

Merke: Das *simple past* wird bereits durch das *did* angezeigt, daher steht das folgende Vollverb in der Grundform (Infinitiv ohne *to*).

Fragen und Verneinungen im *simple past* kannst du ausführlicher auch im Kapitel 6.1 üben.

WISSEN

ÜBUNG 7 **Finde die 12 unregelmäßigen *simple past*-Formen im Wortgitter, trage sie in dein Übungsheft ein und schreibe jeweils rechts daneben die Grundform.**

U	P	A	T	S	U	O	S	N	M	B	Y	C	A	Z
L	V	W	B	U	I	L	T	I	H	J	G	B	Y	B
V	Q	K	R	S	X	N	O	L	J	D	D	O	K	E
X	D	Y	R	B	T	W	O	X	C	R	B	U	F	A
F	R	E	Q	F	D	E	D	J	H	E	Z	G	Z	L
H	A	Z	C	M	W	D	L	K	H	W	V	H	P	M
G	N	A	P	R	O	D	E	C	G	B	O	T	S	Y
O	K	I	Q	W	J	F	K	V	I	X	R	N	U	U
R	N	D	G	N	C	O	U	L	D	P	Q	O	F	A
E	V	S	P	M	L	C	O	X	R	Q	G	B	D	T
Y	T	K	N	E	W	N	D	O	Y	T	A	C	I	Z
U	U	M	M	K	O	E	W	S	R	A	V	B	D	E
Z	A	N	L	X	T	G	W	R	O	T	E	T	C	S
V	F	O	U	N	D	H	G	I	J	F	G	Z	D	A
J	K	K	F	L	I	J	S	M	F	E	Q	D	F	R

ÜBUNG 8 **Bilde wie im Beispiel aus den Satzteilen Fragen und beantworte sie dann einmal bejaht und einmal verneint. Schreibe in dein Übungsheft.**

Beispiel: Did they come to the party? → Yes, they came to the party. / No, they didn't come to the party.

to go to the shop – they

to lose her purse – Tina

~~come to the party – they~~

to clean the room – they

to drink a milk shake – you

to buy a book – Sandra

ÜBEN

ÜBUNG 9 **Übersetze die folgenden Sätze. Schreibe sie in dein Übungsheft.**

1. Tom und Tina waren glücklich.
2. Meine Familie hatte einen großen Hund.
3. Es war sehr lustig.
4. Gestern waren wir zu Hause.
5. Er hatte eine Erkältung.
6. Letzten Montag war ich krank.
7. Letzten Sommer arbeitete Frank im Zoo.

ÜBUNG 10 **In Marys Tagebuch fehlen die richtigen Verbformen. Höre dir Track 4 auf der CD an und fülle die Lücken mit der passenden *simple past*-Form der Verben im Wortspeicher. Überprüfe anschließend dein Ergebnis, in dem du dir nochmals Track 4 anhörst.**

4

to do – to visit – to have to – to have – to know – to be – to be – to be – to help – to get up – to give – to run – cannot – not to have to – to play – to go – to go – to have – to buy – to eat – to write – to drink – to watch – to wake up

On Monday, I ______ my friend Susan. She ______ ill. I ______ her with her homework, but she ______ all the answers herself (selbst). Her mother ______ us some drinks and some sandwiches. In the evening, I ______ Monopoly with my brother. I ______ to bed early, but I ______ sleep. On Tuesday, I ______ to see the dentist (Zahnarzt) because I ______ some problems with my teeth. After that my mother ______ me a new shirt. On Wednesday, I ______ an English test. In the afternoon I ______ my homework. Then I ______ some chocolate and ______ some tea. In the evening, I ______ a film about Africa. On Thursday, I ______ at 7:30 a.m. I ______ late, so I ______ to school. I really ______ hurry! On Friday, I ______ to school because our teacher ______ ill. She ______ a bad cold, just like Susan on Monday. So I ______ at 10 a.m.

ÜBEN

3.3 Das *past progressive*

Die Bildung des *past progressive*

Im Englischen gibt es für das *simple present* eine Verlaufsform, das *present progressive*. Das Gleiche gilt für das *simple past*: Seine Verlaufsform heißt *past progressive*.	The phone rings. The phone **is ringing**. They listened to music. They **were listening** to music.
So bildest du das *past progressive*: *was / were* + Infinitiv (ohne *to*) + *-ing*	It was raining. They were doing the dishes.

Die Verwendung des *past progressive*

Das *past progressive* drückt aus, dass eine Handlung in der Vergangenheit gerade im Verlauf und zum damaligen Zeitpunkt noch nicht abgeschlossen war.	I was playing football when my mum called me to dinner The birds were singing in the trees.
Du verwendest das *past progressive*, wenn ■ du den **Ablauf** einer Handlung betonen möchtest, der einen ganzen Zeitraum ausfüllte, ■ eine **Handlung ablief** (Hintergrundhandlung), während eine weitere (vergangene) Handlung im *simple past* einsetzte.	 He was writing letters from 7 till 10. She was watching TV when the bell rang. I woke up because the phone was ringing.

Vergleich *simple past* und *past progressive*

past progressive: ■ Handlungsabläufe in einem bestimmten Zeitraum, ■ eine bereits andauernde Handlung („Hintergrundhandlung")	 I was cleaning my bike all Sunday morning. I was dancing in the room when somebody knocked at the door.
simple past: ■ Einzelhandlungen, die abgeschlossen sind, ■ aufeinander folgende Handlungen	 Jane wrote an e-mail. She went shopping, then she met Ann.

ÜBUNG 11 **Der folgende Text beinhaltet *simple past* und *past progressive*. Unterstreiche das *simple past* in Rot und das *past progressive* in Blau.**

Last Sunday we had dinner. After dinner we played a game and talked about the day. We went to bed early. While we were listening to the concert, they stole my bike. Ellen was walking home when she met Dennis. His friends were waiting in the kitchen while Tom was cleaning his room.

ÜBUNG 12 **Was passiert auf den Bildern? Bilde Sätze mit der *past progressive*-Form.**

Sandra ______________________.

Tina ______________________.

Rick ______________________.

They ______________________.

Tim ______________________.

Sarah and Jane ______________________.

WISSEN

Signalwörter für das *past progressive*
Hintergrundhandlungen werden oft mit *while (während)* eingeleitet. Für die plötzlich einsetzende Handlung im *simple past* kann *when (als)* verwendet werden.

Achtung: In einem Satz darf immer nur eins von beiden stehen! *While* kann auch für zwei gleichzeitig ablaufende Handlungen eingesetzt werden.

while + past progressive:
While Francis **was waiting** for the bus, it started to rain.
Anna **was having** dinner **while** Charles **was cleaning** the kitchen.

when + simple past:
When the strange man **entered** the room, everybody was talking.

ÜBUNG 13 **Fülle die Lücken mit der richtigen Zeitform – *past progressive* oder *simple past*?**

I ______ (to eat) a sandwich when the phone ______ (to ring).
When Tina ______ (to enter) the restaurant, her family ______ (to wait) there.
While they ______ (to sit) in the waiting room, the door ______ (to open) and an old lady ______ (to come) in.
Mum ______ (to come) home while I ______ (to play) with our dog. Ryan ______ (to do) his homework when Mr Miller ______ (to call).

ÜBUNG 14 **Die Satzteile stehen in der richtigen Reihenfolge. Bilde daraus zusammenhängende Sätze mit der richtigen Zeit und schreibe sie in dein Übungsheft.**

while / Kitty / to have / a shower / Marc / to come / home
I / to play / volleyball / when / Harry / to tell / me / the news
George and Emily / to laugh / when / the taxi / to arrive
The boys / to play / football / while / the girls / to skate / in the park
Mr Stevenson / to talk / to his friend / when / he / to see / the accident

ÜBUNG 15 **Übersetze.**

Mr Miller ging über die Straße, als der Unfall passierte.

______

Während sie im Garten spielte, begann es zu regnen.

______

Tom und Philipp machten Hausaufgaben, während Mrs Jones kochte.

______

Ich schrieb gerade einen Brief an Oma, als der Briefträger *(postman)* an der Tür klingelte.

______

3.4 Das *present perfect*

Das einfache Perfekt (*present perfect*) beschreibt eine Handlung oder ein Ereignis, das bis in die Gegenwart hineinwirkt.

The Smiths **have lived** here for five years (→ sie leben immer noch hier).
Eve **has** just **eaten** a sandwich (→ sie ist jetzt satt).
Greg **has opened** the window (→ das Fenster ist jetzt offen).

Das *present perfect* bei regelmäßigen Verben

So wird das *present perfect* mit regelmäßigen Verben gebildet:
have / has + past participle (3. Verbform)

Marc and John have played volleyball for two hours now.
Judy has played the piano since 5 o'clock.

Das *past participle* bei regelmäßigen Verben ist das Partizip der Vergangenheit und wird wie die *simple past*-Form der regelmäßigen Verben gebildet (↑ Kap. 3.1).

to walk → walked → has / have walked
to call → called → has / have called
to jump → jumped → has / have jumped

Das *present perfect* bei unregelmäßigen Verben

Wie im *simple past* gibt es auch im *present perfect* unregelmäßige Verbformen, für die es keine festen Regeln gibt. Präge sie dir gut ein und lerne sie auswendig. Eine Übersicht über die wichtigsten unregelmäßigen Verben findest du auf Seite 52!

to do → done
I have done everything.
to write → written
My father has written a letter to grandma.
to eat → eaten
Gina has just eaten the cake.
to go → gone
I have gone to school.

Die *present perfect*-Form des **Hilfsverbs** *must* lautet *have had to*.

I have had to do the shopping.

Achtung: Von dem Hilfsverb *can* gibt es keine *present perfect*-Form! Du musst die Ersatzform von *to be able to – können / to be allowed to – dürfen* verwenden.

I have been able to carry these bags.
They haven't been allowed to go to the cinema.

Die Verwendung des *present perfect*

Signalwörter zeigen dir an, wann du das *present perfect* einsetzen musst.

Eine Handlung oder ein Ereignis ist gerade eben abgeschlossen worden:
just – gerade eben

Simon has **just** listened to his new CD.
I have **just** finished my homework.

Eine Handlung oder ein Ereignis begann in der Vergangenheit und dauert bis in die Gegenwart an:
since / for – seit

Anna has lived here **for** ten years.
She has lived here **since** 1999.

Eine Handlung oder ein Ereignis fand in der Vergangenheit statt, aber die Zeit wird nicht genau angegeben. Die Handlung selbst ist wichtig, nicht der Zeitpunkt:
already – schon
not ... yet – noch nicht

I have **already** seen the film.
I have**n't** been to the new shopping centre **yet.**

Die **Signalwörter** für das *present perfect* haben eine feste Stellung im Satz:

- Unmittelbar **vor** dem *past participle* stehen:
  never – niemals *ever – jemals*
  already – schon *always – immer*
  just – gerade eben *often – oft*

Victoria has **already** packed.
He has **always** liked hamburgers.
I have **just** written a letter.

- Immer am **Satzende** stehen:
  before – vorher *(not ...) yet – noch nicht*
  so far – bisher

Victor has not packed **yet.**
Have you been to Scotland **before?**

- **Vor der Zeitangabe** stehen:
  since / for – seit

Margret has worked here **for** five months.
I have not seen my uncle **since** May.

Die **Verneinung** wird mit *not* gebildet, das immer nach *have / has* steht.

Have you seen my glasses? – No, I have not / haven't seen them.

Zur Bildung von **Fragen** im *present perfect*: ↑ Kap. 6.2!

Have you had lunch already?

ÜBUNG 16 **Hier sind verschiedene Verbformen durcheinander geraten: Grundform, *simple past* und *past participle*. Unterstreiche alle Formen, die *past participle* sein können:**

eaten – drink – thought – shown – sang – spoke – driven – eat – gone – done – break – have – knew – were – write – written – fall – keep – know – drunk – slept – show – ring – rung – begin – begun – been – was – stolen – became – laugh – rang – taken – met

ÜBUNG 17 **Bilde die passende *present perfect*-Form: Trage sie in das Wortgitter ein und löse das Buchstabenrätsel.**

1. to stop / he	5. to cycle / he	9. to pull / he	13. to love / we
2. to watch / we	6. to allow / she	10. to live / I	14. to dance / he
3. to try / you	7. to look / she	11. to wash / she	
4. to laugh / he	8. to close / we	12. to worry / they	

1 H E H A S S T O P P E D
2
3
4
5
6
7
8
9
10
11
12
13
14

with the dogs.

ÜBUNG 18 **Höre dir Track 5 auf der CD an und setze das *present perfect* ein.**

5

Ida's bike is shining. She ______ just ______ it.

______ you ______ your homework? – Yes, I ______ already ______ it.

Jim ______ take his medicine.

Look here, my hands are clean. I ______ just ______ them.

We have English at school. I ______ it for two years.

Marc ______ in Berlin for three years now.

We ______ to France yet.

Jane and Tim ______ the magazines. They don't need them anymore.

ÜBUNG 19 **Trage die Übersetzung der Signalwörter für das *present perfect* in das Gitter ein.**

1. seit (Zeitpunkt)
2. niemals
3. schon
4. seit (Zeitraum)
5. jemals
6. noch nicht

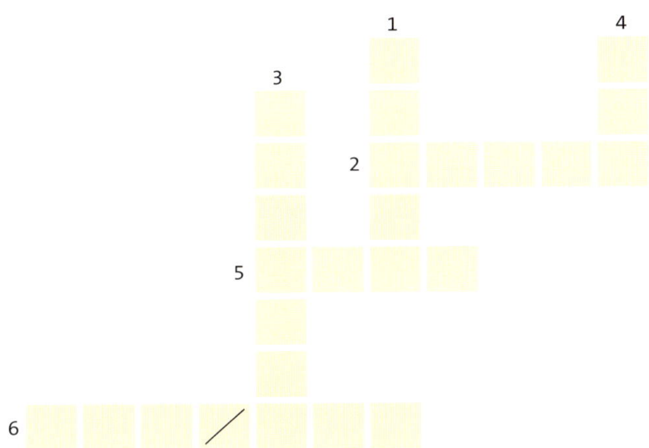

ÜBUNG 20 **Signalwörter zeigen dir, dass das *present perfect* verwendet werden muss. Achte auf die Satzstellung und bilde einen passenden Satz! Schreibe die Lösungen in dein Übungsheft.**

just: Gina / to write / a letter
never: I / to listen / to Indian music
for: Harry and Kim / to work / in a restaurant / nine months
already: we / can *(können)* book our trip / to Paris *(Ersatzform verwenden)*
not yet: He / can *(dürfen)* go / to London *(Ersatzform verwenden)*

ÜBEN

ÜBUNG 21 **Übersetze und schreibe in dein Übungsheft.**

Sie haben gerade ihre Arbeit beendet.
Sie hat gerade die Fenster geputzt.
Rosa lebt seit zwei Jahren in Rom *(Rome)*.
Ich habe die CD schon angehört.

WISSEN

Since* und *for* im *present perfect
Since und *for* sind eindeutige Signalwörter für das *present perfect*. Sie zeigen an, dass etwas in der Vergangenheit begonnen hat und in der Gegenwart noch andauert.

Achtung: Im Deutschen wird häufig das Präsens verwendet: I **have lived** in England for eight years. → Ich **lebe** seit acht Jahren in England.

since → **Zeitpunkt:**
Since zeigt an, wann eine Handlung oder ein Ereignis angefangen hat: since Monday, since 1947, since 8 o'clock.

for → **Zeitraum:**
For zeigt an, wie lange eine Handlung oder ein Ereignis bereits andauert: for two weeks, for six years, for a long time

ÜBUNG 22 **Zeitpunkt oder Zeitraum? Ordne die Zeitangaben der richtigen Spalte zu und schreibe jeweils *since* oder *for* dazu.**

two years – yesterday – one hour – 1984 – last October – ten months – the last two weeks – 9 o'clock – Friday – January 1st – Christmas – a long time – six days – one minute

***since* (Zeitpunkt)**	***for* (Zeitraum)**

ÜBEN

ÜBUNG 23 **Die folgenden Sätze beschreiben, was einige Personen gerade tun *(present progressive)*. Setze die Handlungen ins *present perfect*. Schreibe in dein Übungsheft.**

Beispiel: They are taking the dog for a walk. → They have taken the dog for a walk.

She is writing a birthday card.
He is making his bed.
I am doing my homework.
The dogs are eating the cake.
Michael is listening to the new CD.
My friends are buying a present.
Grandmother is reading the newspaper.

ÜBUNG 24 **Formuliere ganze Sätze mithilfe der Stichwörter.**

1.

2.

3.

4.

5.

1. Frank looks unhappy (to lose, mobile phone).

   He has lost his mobile phone.

2. David and Peter are very tired (to walk, all the way home).

3. Ralph has got chocolate around his mouth (to eat, chocolate cake).

4. The car is damaged (Ruth, to have, accident).

5. Eric doesn't talk to me (I, to forget, birthday).

ÜBUNG 25 **Bilde Sätze im *present perfect* und entscheide, ob du *since* oder *for* benötigst. Schreibe die Sätze in dein Übungsheft.**

I / to eat / Chinese food / I was 10 years old
Julia and Ron / to know / each other / 2007
the girls / to talk / on the phone / three hours

ÜBUNG 26 **Höre dir Track 6 auf der CD an und setze in die Lücken die richtige Form des *present perfect* ein.**

6

The Greens and the Sanders are planning to go to the adventure park.

It's 8 o'clock in the morning.

Gina Green: "Mum, dad, wake up! We ______. I ______ the alarm clock. Lisa ______ just ______. The Sanders ______ already ______."

(later)

Dad: "I ______ the picnic. ______ you ______ a shower, Gina?"

Gina: "Yes, I ______ just ______ in the bathroom. It's your turn now. ______ you ______ some biscuits and a bottle of water?"

Dad: "Yes, I ______ everything in the bag. But I ______ our swimsuits."

Mum: "I ______ just ______ them on the table over there.

Gina: "Listen, the phone is ringing! … *(a moment later)* Lisa ______ again. The Sanders ______ back home because they ______ their money."

ÜBUNG 27 **Übersetze die folgenden Sätze. Schreibe sie in dein Übungsheft.**

Ich habe das Buch schon gelesen.
Meine Mutter hat gerade eben angerufen.
Kate spielt seit vier Jahren Golf.
Richard hat schon Blumen gekauft.

ÜBEN

3.5 Zeitformen der Vergangenheit im Vergleich

Wie im Deutschen gibt es im Englischen mehrere Zeitformen für die Vergangenheit:

- Ist eine Handlung in der Vergangenheit abgeschlossen, steht das *simple past*.
  Yesterday I went for a walk.
- Wird der Handlungsablauf in der Vergangenheit betont, verwendest du das *past progressive*.
  He was working all day long.
- Hat die Handlung eine Nachwirkung bis in die Gegenwart, benutze das *present perfect*.
  Karen has learned English since April.

Simple past und *past progressive*

Wird der **Zeitpunkt** *(→ simple past)* oder der **Zeitraum** *(→ past progressive)* betont?

Warren wrote a letter yesterday.
Victoria was singing the whole day.

Begann eine Handlung vor einer anderen? → Die bereits andauernde Handlung steht im *past progressive*, die neu einsetzende Handlung im *simple past*.

We were having a party when my mother came home.
While Lisa was cooking, Aunt Helen arrived.

Simple past und *present perfect*

Ist die Handlung in der Vergangenheit komplett **abgeschlossen** und hat jetzt in der Gegenwart keine Bedeutung mehr, steht das *simple past*.

I did my homework on Monday.
She was unhappy yesterday.

Begann die Handlung in der Vergangenheit und **dauert bis jetzt an** oder hat jetzt noch einen Bezug zur Gegenwart, so muss das *present perfect* stehen.
Abgeschlossene Handlung → *simple past*,
Gegenwartsbezug → *present perfect*.

Sabrina has lived here for two months.
Tom has just finished the book.

Aufgepasst: Im Deutschen kann man verschiedene Vergangenheitsformen für die gleiche Situation verwenden, im Englischen nicht.

Gestern habe ich neue CDs gekauft. = Gestern kaufte ich neue CDs.
aber nur: I **bought** some CDs **yesterday.**

Wichtige unregelmäßige Verben *(irregular verbs)*

infinitive	*simple past*	*past participle*	*deutsche Bedeutung*
to be	was / were	been	sein
to begin	began	begun	anfangen
to break	broke	broken	zerbrechen
to buy	bought	bought	kaufen
to catch	caught	caught	fangen
to come	came	come	kommen
to do	did	done	machen, tun
to drink	drank	drunk	trinken
to drive	drove	driven	(Auto) fahren
to eat	ate	eaten	essen
to fall	fell	fallen	fallen
to find	found	found	finden
to forget	forgot	forgotten	vergessen
to get	got	got	bekommen
to give	gave	given	geben
to go	went	gone	gehen
to have	had	had	haben
to hear	heard	heard	hören
to know	knew	known	kennen, wissen
to leave	left	left	verlassen
to lose	lost	lost	verlieren
to make	made	made	machen
to meet	met	met	treffen
to pay	paid	paid	bezahlen
to run	ran	run	laufen
to say	said	said	sagen
to see	saw	seen	sehen
to sell	sold	sold	verkaufen
to send	sent	sent	schicken
to show	showed	shown	zeigen
to stand	stood	stood	stehen
to take	took	taken	nehmen
to teach	taught	taught	unterrichten
to tell	told	told	erzählen
to think	thought	thought	denken
to win	won	won	gewinnen
to write	wrote	written	schreiben

ÜBUNG 28 **Im Wortspeicher ist alles durcheinandergeraten: *simple past-*, *past progressive-* und *present perfect*-Formen. Ordne richtig in die Tabelle ein.**

threw – have drawn – was eating – went – were going – has gone – were doing – listened – was cleaning – has bought – have seen – visited – lost – has slept – did – was wearing – have told – were having

simple past	*past progressive*	*present perfect*

ÜBUNG 29 **Hier hast du einige rätselhafte Sätze. Trage die Vergangenheitsform als Überschrift ein und bilde aus den durcheinander geratenen Buchstaben die richtige Verbform. Schreibe die richtigen Sätze in dein Übungsheft. Ein Tipp: Die Grundformen der Verben stehen am Ende der Sätze.**

Gina GCAWWTHISAN TV and Andrew TASTWINGIS next to her. (to watch, to sit).
While they IRGEEALKWWN home, a bus passed them. (to walk)

At 8 o'clock I TEA some bread, RKAND a cup of tea and OKOT the bus. (to eat, to drink, to take)

Uncle John TAWRHTESIN six postcards since he left. (to write)
I HEVA just TEDRUN off the radio. (to turn)

ÜBEN

ÜBUNG 30 **Die Wörterschlange hat immer die gleiche Reihenfolge: *infinitive – simple past – present perfect – infinitive – simple past* usw. Fülle die Lücken richtig aus.**

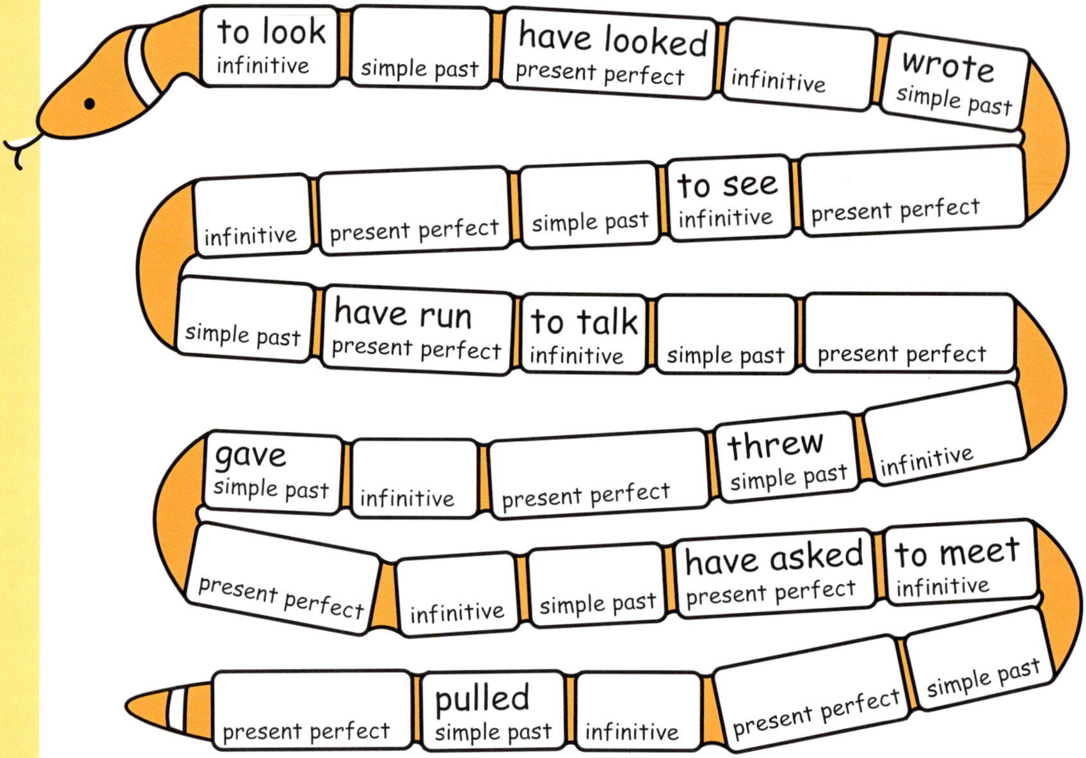

ÜBUNG 31 **Nun musst du dich entscheiden: *simple past* oder *present perfect*? Achte auf die Signalwörter.**

Last Christmas we ________ (to have) turkey (*Truthahn*) for dinner.

Sarah ________ (to write) the e-mail two weeks ago.

Grandma ________ just ________ (to arrive).

Max and Tina ________ (to go) to England last year.

Dana ________ (to be) to England ________ (since / for) three months.

Mum ________ (to wear) her new dress last Sunday.

Victor ________ never ________ (to wear) his new jeans so far.

The Millers ________ (to paint) their house in March. It is pink and yellow now.

ÜBEN

ÜBUNG 32 **Setze *simple past, past progressive* oder *present perfect* ein. Achte auf alle Signalwörter und den Zeitraum oder Zeitpunkt der Handlung!**

1. Yesterday Gina _____ (to eat) pizza for dinner.
   Rachel _____ (to eat) pizza for the last three days.
   I _____ (to eat) pizza when Eddy _____ (to come) along.
2. While Emma _____ (to walk) to school, she _____ (to meet) Sam.
   I _____ (to walk) home yesterday.
   She _____ just _____ (to walk) through the door.
3. He _____ just _____ (to write) the letter.
   I _____ (to write) a postcard when the phone _____ (to ring).
   They _____ (to write) an e-mail two weeks ago.

ÜBUNG 33 **Bilde einen Satz mit einer Hintergrundhandlung und einem plötzlich einsetzenden Ereignis. Verwende immer abwechselnd beim ersten Satz *when*, beim zweiten Satz *while*. Schreibe in dein Übungsheft.**

Hintergrundhandlung	**plötzlich einsetzendes Ereignis**
Fred – to have breakfast	suddenly – the fire alarm – to start
Fred was having breakfast when suddenly the fire alarm started.	
we – to sit in the park	a dog – to jump – at us
While …	
they – to work in the garden	a mouse – to run – through the bushes
Joan – to sell clothes in a shop	someone – to steal – a shirt
I – to ride my bike – in the forest	a rabbit – to cross – my path
they – to take pictures	the battery – to die
Liz – to watch a film	someone – to scream
Sally – to read the newspapers	suddenly – her Dad's name – to discover

Klassenarbeit 1

45 Minuten

AUFGABE 1 **Handelt es sich bei den folgenden Sätzen um *simple past, past progressive* oder *present perfect*? Kreuze an. Unterstreiche das Signalwort.**

	simple past	past progressive	present perfect
Father has just arrived here.	☐	☐	☐
Verena bought a new board two weeks ago.	☐	☐	☐
I have learned English for two years.	☐	☐	☐
While the baby was playing, its mother ...	☐	☐	☐
Have you ever seen a Shakespeare play?	☐	☐	☐
We walked all the way to the city centre on Monday.	☐	☐	☐
Tony has played the piano for one hour.	☐	☐	☐

AUFGABE 2 **Ergänze die fehlenden Formen.**

Grundform	***simple past***	***past participle***
to run		
	bought	
		been
to think		
		written
	knew	
to leave		
to speak		
		told
to meet		
	stood	
to win		
		gotten
	gave	
		done

AUFGABE 3 **Entscheide dich – setze *simple past* oder *past progressive* ein.**

While Lena ____________ (to sleep), the dog suddenly ____________ (to bark).

Rosa ____________ (to sit) at the lake when someone ____________ (to scream).

While Mrs Turner ____________ (to wait) for the bus and Tina ____________ (to talk) to her best friend, an accident ____________ (to happen).

They ____________ (to eat) ice cream when the thief ____________ (to take) the bag.

I ____________ (to read) a book and my brother ____________ (to study).

The boys ____________ (to play) cards when the bell ____________ (to ring).

AUFGABE 4 **Signalwörter zeigen dir, welche Zeitform du verwenden musst. Ordne sie der richtigen Zeitform in der Tabelle zu.**

yesterday – so far – last week – since last July – one week ago – for two days – never – in 1983 – last year – just – already – last summer

Signalwörter für *simple past*	Signalwörter für *present perfect*

AUFGABE 5 **Formuliere kurze Merksätze. Wann verwendet man *simple past*, *past progressive* oder *present perfect?* Nenne Signalwörter.**

past progressive:
Das *past progressive* wird verwendet, um den ________ einer Handlung zu betonen.
Signalwörter sind: w________, w________

simple past:
Das *simple past* wird verwendet, wenn eine Handlung in der ________ abgeschlossen ist.
Signalwörter sind: y________, l________ y________, one w________ a________

present perfect:
Das *present perfect* wird verwendet, wenn eine Handlung in der ________ begonnen hat und in der ________ noch von Bedeutung ist.
Signalwörter sind: s________, f________, j________, alr________, y________

AUFGABE 6 **Setze die fehlende Zeitform ein. Entscheide dich zwischen *simple past*, *past progressive* oder *present perfect*.**

Susan and Lisa ________ (to ride) their bikes when the rain ________ (to start).
Benny ________ (to learn) three languages ________ (since / for) 2001.
My friends ________ just ________ (to arrive) at the restaurant.
Leonardo da Vinci ________ (to paint) the Mona Lisa in 1503.
The girls ________ (to talk) to each other while the boys ________ (to play) with the dogs.
I ________ (to buy) the tomatoes three days ago.
The family ________ (to live) in America ________ (since / for) ten years now.
Mrs George ________ already ________ (to read) three books by John Steinbeck.

TESTEN

Klassenarbeit 2

60 Minuten

AUFGABE 7 **Nenne, zu welcher englischen Zeit die folgenden Verbformen gehören.**

was / were + *ing*-Form des Verbs →

am / are / is + *ing*-Form des Verbs →

personal pronoun + *past participle* →

had been + *ing*-Form des Verbs →

AUFGABE 8 **Setze die angegeben Verben in die richtige Form.**

he / to drink / *simple past* →

they / to see / *past progressive* →

we / to have / *simple past* →

she / to read / *present progressive* →

I / to watch / *simple past* →

you / to leave / *past progressive* →

AUFGABE 9 ***Present perfect simple.*** **Schreibe vollständige Sätze.**

Mary / to finish / her homework

Mr Miller / to wash / his car

Lilly / to write / a letter

The guest / to eat / a delicious meal

Grandma / to bake / a cake

AUFGABE 10 ***Present perfect* oder *simple past*? Schreibe zuerst eine Frage, dann die passende Antwort in dein Übungsheft.**

Beispiel: to be to Hollywood / yes / to go there in 2006 → Have you ever been to Hollywood? Yes, I have. I went there in 2006.

ever / to swim in the Atlantic Ocean / yes / last year
ever / to play beach volleyball / no
ever / to go skiing / yes / last Christmas
ever / to ride a mountainbike / yes / last summer in Switzerland
ever / to drink champagne / yes / on my 14th birthday
ever / to lose a pair of shoes / yes / last summer

AUFGABE 11 **Mixed tenses. Schreibe die richtigen Formen in die Lücken. Achte auf die korrekte Zeit.**

Mother came in to Mia's room while she ______ (to cry).

What are you doing at the moment? – I ______ (to wash) the dishes.

While Laura ______ (to wait) for her school bus, she ______ (to see) an accident happen.

When Hannah ______ (to be) a little girl, her family ______ (to live) in New Zealand for three years.

The sun ______ (to rise) every morning.

Lilly ______ (to finish) her homework before her father came home.

Mother ______ (to visit) grandmother in hospital twice since last Friday.

Two years ago, while John ______ (to travel) through Australia, an earthquake happened.

AUFGABE 12 **Übersetze. Schreibe in dein Übungsheft.**

Meine Schwester lebt seit zwei Jahren in Irland.
War Laura gestern auf Peters Party?
Mary spielt seit fünf Jahren Klavier.
Wer hat dir denn diese Geschichte erzählt?
Ich bin gestern ins Kino gegangen und habe Eis gegessen.

Klassenarbeit 3

60 Minuten

AUFGABE 13 **Gib vom jeweiligen Verb die angegebene Form an.**

to keep / *simple present* →

to forget / *past participle* →

to put / *past participle* →

to ride / *simple past* →

to ride / *past participle* →

to buy / *simple past* →

to eat / *simple past* →

to do / *past participle* →

AUFGABE 14 **Sarah erzählt von ihrem letzten Campingurlaub. Setze das angegebene Verb in die richtige Form.**

A year ago my friends and I ______ (to take) the train to Scotland. We ______ (to go) with other children from our youth club. Tessa and I ______ (to organise) the holiday. Our club leader ______ (to help), of course. We ______ (to stay) in tents. We ______ (to cook) our own meals. We ______ (to walk) to a lot of interesting places there. We ______ (to have) a lot of fun. I really ______ (to like) last year's holidays!

AUFGABE 15 ***Simple past* oder *past progressive*?**

When Peter's mother ______ (to come) into Peter's room she ______ (to see) that he and his friends ______ (to play) a computer game. She ______ (to tell) them to stop. Peter, however, ______ (to tell) his mother that they ______ (to play) a harmless game and ______ (to ask) his mother to leave his room. Peter's mother ______ (to get) very angry. She ______ (to leave) the room, but ______ (to give) her son a fierce glance.

AUFGABE 16 **Formuliere Fragen. Frage nach den unterstrichenen Satzgliedern. Schreibe in dein Übungsheft.**

Mary read a book <u>last night</u>.
Last summer, Lisa travelled <u>to Spain</u>.
Sarah took <u>Jamie's</u> book.
<u>Somebody</u> stole my bike.
Last Friday night, I stayed at home <u>because I had a fever</u>.
I want to speak <u>to Mary</u>.
Megan saw <u>a dead rat</u>.

AUFGABE 17 **Formuliere ganze Sätze. Verwende immer das *past progressive*.**

Last Saturday, ...

the dog / to chase / the cat

Mr Miller / to wash / the dishes

the children / to watch / TV

the sun / to shine

... when the telephone rang and Mrs Miller's sister called from New Zealand.

AUFGABE 18 **Formuliere zu den Sätzen aus Aufgabe 17 die passenden Fragen. Schreibe in dein Übungsheft.**

AUFGABE 19 ***Simple past* oder *past progressive*? Schreibe vollständige Sätze in dein Übungsheft.**

While the Millers / to watch TV / a burglar / to break into / their garage.
Grandma Elisabeth / to clean / the kitchen window / to see / an accident. She / to go / to the phone / to call / the police.
Maggie / to do her homework / when / to hear / a strange noise. She / to look outside / and / see / the hail *(Hagel)*.

4.1 Das *will-future*

Die Bildung des *will-future*

Im Englischen gibt es mehrere Möglichkeiten, die Zukunft auszudrücken, unter anderem das *will-future* und das *going to-future*.

Das *will-future* wird mit ***will*** und dem **Infinitiv** (ohne *to*) gebildet.

Aussage: *will* + Infinitiv (ohne *to*)	Anna will marry one day.
Verneinung: *will* + *not* + Infinitiv (ohne *to*)	Anna will not marry one day.
Frage: *will*-Form vor das *Subjekt* stellen	Will Anna marry one day?

Die Verwendung des *will-future*

Das *will future* wird verwendet bei

■ unbeeinflussbaren Ereignissen und Zuständen in der Zukunft,	It will be warm tomorrow. (→ Das Wetter kann niemand beeinflussen.) It will be Sarah's birthday next Monday. (→ Daran kann niemand etwas ändern.)
■ Vermutungen, Hoffnungen und Voraussagen,	I think she will call me. (→ Du vermutest, dass sie anrufen wird.) I hope we will have fun. (→ Du hoffst, dass ihr eine lustige Zeit miteinander verbringen werdet.)
■ spontanen Entscheidungen für die nahe Zukunft,	You look hungry. I will make you a sandwich. (→ Du fällst eine spontane Entscheidung.)
■ Bedingungssätzen mit *if* (↑ Kap. 5.3).	If you run, you will reach the bus. (→ Bedingung: Du musst rennen; Folge: Du wirst den Bus erreichen.)

ÜBUNG 1 **Höre dir Track 7 auf der CD an und setze das *will-future* ein.**

7

1. **Unbeeinflussbare Ereignisse und Zustände in der Zukunft**

   We have tickets for the cinema. We ______ you later.

   We must go now or we ______ the bus.

2. **Vermutungen, Hoffnungen und Voraussagen**

   Don't eat so much chocolate. You ______ fat.

   I think Manchester United ______ the football match.

3. **Spontane Entscheidungen für die nahe Zukunft**

   Do you need sugar? Wait, I ______ some.

   You look unhappy. I ______.

4. **Verwendung in Bedingungssätzen mit *if***

   If I get a mountain bike, we ______ on a cycling holiday.

   If I don't find the way, I ______ a policeman.

ÜBUNG 2 **Formuliere selbst Sätze zu den vier Verwendungsmöglichkeiten des *will-future* (siehe Übung 1). Beachte die Satzstellung Subjekt – Verb – Objekt und schreibe in dein Übungsheft.**

1. It's snowing. – a traffic jam / in the evening / to be / there
2. Tomorrow there's a party at Lisa's. – come / to the party / John / too
3. Stop! There is an accident. – to call / I / the police
4. If the weather is bad, – not / to play / we / in the garden

WISSEN +

Die Kurzform des *will-future*
Du hast bisher nur die **Langform** des *will-future (will/will not)* kennen gelernt. Häufig wird auch die **Kurzform** benutzt. Die Kurzform wird eher beim Sprechen verwendet, die Langform meist beim Schreiben.

will + Infinitiv (ohne *to*) → *'ll*
Wait, I'll get some sugar.
We'll see you tomorrow.

will + *not* + Infinitiv (ohne *to*) → *won't*
I won't go.
We won't ask him.

ÜBEN

ÜBUNG 3 **Setze die fehlende *will*-Form (Langform) ein und kreuze an, welche der vier Verwendungsmöglichkeiten (siehe Übung 1) vorliegt.**

	(1)	(2)	(3)	(4)
Okay, we ______ (to do) it right now.	☐	☐	☐	☐
I'm ill. I hope my friend ______ (to visit) me.	☐	☐	☐	☐
If I meet them, I ______ (to tell) them.	☐	☐	☐	☐
Don't worry, we ______ (to help) you.	☐	☐	☐	☐
Tomorrow the weather ______ (to be) fine.	☐	☐	☐	☐
I'm sure Tim ______ (not/to be) angry.	☐	☐	☐	☐

WISSEN

Signalwörter helfen
Vermutungen und Hoffnungen, bei denen das *will-future* verwendet wird, sind oft gekennzeichnet durch *Signalwörter* wie:

I think – ich glaube
I suppose – ich vermute
I hope – ich hoffe
I am sure – ich bin sicher
perhaps – vielleicht
probably – wahrscheinlich

ÜBUNG 4 **Wie wirst du in 25 Jahren leben? Formuliere Hoffnungen und Voraussagen über dein zukünftiges Leben, indem du die Stichwörter benutzt.**

Beispiel: hope: rich / happy → I hope I will be rich and happy.

think: travel / around the world
sure: live / big house
suppose: look / like / film star
perhaps: president / Germany

ÜBUNG 5 **Übersetze. Schreibe die Sätze in dein Übungsheft.**

Wir glauben, Phil kommt morgen.
Wird es nicht regnen?
Morgen wirst du vielleicht meinen Freund sehen.
Falls das Geschäft öffnet, werden wir einkaufen.
Ich werde nicht zu Simons Party gehen.

4.2 Das *going to-future*

Die Bildung des *going to-future*

Auch mit dem *going to-future* kann man ein zukünftiges Ereignis ausdrücken. Es wird mit einer Form von ***to be*** und ***going to*** und dem **Infinitiv** (ohne *to*) gebildet.	
Aussage: *to be + going to* + Infinitiv (ohne *to*)	We are going to have a party on Saturday.
Verneinung: *to be + not going to* + Infinitiv (ohne *to*)	They are not going to come to our party.
Frage: Hilfsverb *to be* vor das Subjekt stellen	Are you going to wear a shirt for the party?
Für die Bildung des *going to-future* brauchst du die Formen von ***to be***.	Singular: I am, you are, he / she / it is Plural: we are, you are, they are
Aufgepasst: Verwechsle nicht die Verlaufsform der Gegenwart (*present progressive*) mit dem *going to-future*!	I'm going home (Verlaufsform). → Ich gehe gerade nach Hause. *Aber:* I'm going to go home (*going to-future*) → Ich werde nach Hause gehen.

Die Verwendung des *going to-future*

Das *going to-future* wird verwendet bei: ■ festen Vorhaben, Verabredungen, Plänen und bereits gefällten Entscheidungen,	I am going to visit my friend at the weekend. (→ Du hast das fest vor.) These are the ingredients (*Zutaten*). I am going to make a cake. (→ Dein Entschluss steht fest.)
■ Voraussagen, die mit großer Sicherheit eintreten werden oder absehbar sind.	Tom is going to do his homework this afternoon. (→ Wenn nichts dazwischen kommt, wird er seine Hausaufgaben erledigen.) Look, the ladder is broken. Liz is going to fall down. (→ Es ist absehbar, dass Liz herunterfällt, da die Leiter kaputt ist.)

ÜBUNG 6 **Setze die richtigen Formen des *going to-future* ein.**

1. **Feste Vorhaben, Verabredungen, Pläne, gefällte Entscheidungen**

   David ________ (to meet) his father after school.

   I ________ (to stay) at home next weekend.

   Dad ________ (to do) the washing-up after lunch.

   Our teacher promised: we ________ (listen) to pop songs.

2. **Mit großer Sicherheit eintretende oder absehbare Voraussagen**

   Look at the clouds. It ________ (to rain).

   Ann has got a cloth *(Tuch)* in her hand. She ________ (to clean) her bike.

   Aunt Helen called. Sue and Kim ________ (to visit) her tomorrow.

ÜBUNG 7 **Setze die fehlende *going to*-Zukunftsform ein und kreuze an, welche der zwei Anwendungsmöglichkeiten (siehe Übung 6) vorliegt.**

	(1)	(2)
Jim has got toothache. He ________ (to see) the dentist.	☐	☐
Look here. I ________ (to eat) your cookie.	☐	☐
We ________ (to move) to Italy next year.	☐	☐
Look at the ship. It ________ (to sink).	☐	☐
My plans for Saturday: I ________ (to do) a lot of sports.	☐	☐
Jane ________ (not / to come). She had an accident yesterday.	☐	☐

ÜBUNG 8 **Will, Sandra, Dave und Betty haben verschiedene Pläne für das Wochenende. Formuliere Sätze mit dem *going to-future*. Schreibe in dein Übungsheft.**

Beispiel: Ralph is going to clean his bike on Sunday at 7 p.m.

Will	Sandra	Dave	Betty	you
Saturday	Sunday	Saturday	Sunday	Saturday
4 p.m.	9 a.m.	2 p.m.	3 p.m.	11 a.m.
play football	go to the lake	visit Francis	watch Formula 1	?

WISSEN

Die Kurzform des *going to-future*
Beim *going to-future (am / is / are going to)* gibt es wie beim *will-future* eine **Langform** und eine **Kurzform**. Die Kurzform wird eher beim Sprechen verwendet, die Langform meist beim Schreiben.

am → ***'m***	I'm going to eat the cake.
is → ***'s***	He's going to play in the garden.
are → ***'re***	We're going to meet Jill at the station.
am not → ***'m not***	I'm not going to work here.
is not → ***'s not / isn't***	She's not / isn't going to do her homework.
are not → ***'re not / aren't***	They're not / aren't going to ask him.

ÜBUNG 9 **Setze die fehlenden *going to*-Formen ein.**

Pat: "Look at those clouds. It ______ (to rain) soon."

Kim: "Don't worry. We ______ ______ (to reach, *erreichen*) the next village in five minutes. So we ______ (not / to get) wet."

Pat: "That's not right. The next village is three miles away. And look, the first raindrops! We ______ (to get) wet."

Kim: "What ______ (we / to do) now?"

Pat: "Look, there's a shelter *(Unterstand)*. We ______ (to wait) there until the rain stops."

ÜBUNG 10 **Übersetze die Sätze ins Englische und schreibe sie in dein Übungsheft. Überlege dir, ob es sich um ein festes Vorhaben (1) oder eine absehbare Voraussage (2) handelt und schreibe die Zahlen dazu.**

Schau mal, das kleine Mädchen! Sie wird gleich vom Fahrrad fallen *(to fall off)*.
Wirst du deine Ferien in Italien verbringen?
Schau dir die Wolken an! Es wird schneien.
Hier sind die Karten *(tickets)*. Wir werden am Samstag zu dem Open-Air-Konzert gehen.

ÜBEN

4.3 *Will-future* und *going to-future* im Vergleich

Will-future:	
■ unbeeinflussbare Ereignisse	It will be warm and sunny.
■ Vermutungen, Hoffnungen, Voraussagen	I hope she will not be angry.
■ spontane Entscheidungen	I will help you.
→ **wahrscheinlich eintretende Zukunft**	
Going to-future:	
■ feste Vorhaben, Verabredungen, Pläne und bereits gefällte Entscheidungen	He is going to play volleyball on Monday. We are going to see grandma tomorrow.
■ Voraussagen, die mit großer Sicherheit eintreten werden oder absehbar sind	I am not going to pass the exams. Dean is going to win the match on Sunday.
→ **fest geplante Zukunft**	

Besonderheiten

Die **Hilfsverben** *can, may* und *must* dürfen **nicht** mit *will* oder *going to* kombiniert werden!	I will be able to drive a car when I'm 18. I hope I will be allowed to go outside. I will have to go home.
Benutze stattdessen die Ersatzformen *be able to, be allowed to* und *have to* (↑ Kap. 2.2 und 2.3).	
Aufgepasst: Mit *will* wird eine zukünftige Handlung ausgedrückt. Beim deutschen wollen musst du *want to* verwenden.	I will go *(will-future).* → Ich werde gehen. I want to go *(simple present).* – Ich *will* gehen.
Merke: Bei **Fragen** und **Verneinungen** steht niemals *to do*, da bereits ein Hilfsverb vorhanden ist: *will* beim *will-future*, *to be* beim *going to-future*.	Will the weather be nice tomorrow? Are you going to meet Jean on Monday? I hope she will not come. He is not going to come.

ÜBUNG 11 **Wann verwendet man das *will-future* und wann das *going to-future*? Schließe das Buch, schreibe die Verwendungsformen auf ein leeres Blatt und vergleiche deine Antwort dann mit der vorherigen Seite.**

ÜBUNG 12 **Kennzeichne die Sätze, die das *will-future* benötigen, mit *w* und die Aussagen, bei denen das *going to-future* stehen muss, mit *g*.**

Ereignisse, die du nicht beeinflussen kannst: ___

Du hoffst, dass etwas eintritt: ___

Ihr habt einen festen Plan für das kommende Wochenende: ___

Du entscheidest dich ganz spontan, deinem Freund zu helfen: ___

Du beobachtest zwei Autos, die gleich zusammenstoßen werden: ___

Wenn du Arzt bist *(Bedingung!)*, dann wirst du Leben retten: ___

ÜBUNG 13 **Spontane Entscheidung *(will-future)* oder fester Vorsatz *(going to-future)*? Setze die passende Zukunftsform ein.**

Randy: "Look here, my bike. I can't use it, the brakes *(Bremsen)* are not working. My dad ___ (to repair) it on Saturday."

Simon: "Don't wait until Saturday. I ___ (to check) it for you."

Randy: "Thanks a lot. But I need new brakes. Dad and I ___ (to buy) them on Saturday. Do you want to come with us?"

Simon: "Yes, of course, I ___ (to come), too."

WISSEN

***Will-future* und *going to-future* bei Fragen** *will-future:* **Subjekt** und *will* tauschen	**You** *will* go there. → Will **you** go there?
going to-future: **Subjekt** und Hilfsverb *to be* tauschen	**She** *is* going to meet you. → Is **she** going to meet you?
Fragewörter werden bei beiden Formen vorangestellt.	**Where** will you go? **Where** are you going to go on Monday?

ÜBEN

ÜBUNG 14 **Formuliere Fragen in der passenden Zukunftsform.**

(you / to watch) the match on Sunday? – No, I'm not.

(Ralph / to like) my dog? – No, he won't. He hates dogs.

(sun / to shine) tomorrow? – Yes, it will.

(what / you / to do) on Tuesday? – I'm not sure yet.

ÜBUNG 15 **Ruth ist bei einer Wahrsagerin (*fortune teller*). Füge die passende Zukunftsform ein. Überlege genau, ob es sich um eine Vorhersage (*will-future*) oder ein festes Vorhaben (*going to-future*) handelt.**

Fortune teller: "You (to be) happy all your life."

Ruth: "That's nice. I (to have) a party next Sunday. (it / to be) a good party?"

Fortune teller: "Let's see. Yes, it (to be) good. And a nice boy (to come) to the party. His name is Andrew."

Ruth: "Yes, you are right. Andrew (to come). I invited him."

ÜBUNG 16 **Setze entweder *will-future* oder *going to-future* in die Lücken ein.**

What about next Friday? – I (to play) basketball with my friends.

I've got a headache. – Have you? Wait here and I (to get) a glass of water for you.

Why are you filling this bucket with water? – I (to wash) the car.

If you take the dog for a walk, it (to bark) anymore.

It's decided *(entschieden)*, they (to build) a new house. It (to be) very noisy the next months.

Klassenarbeit 1

45 Minuten

AUFGABE 1 **Unterstreiche die Zukunftsformen. Bezeichne die Art der zukünftigen Handlung.**

She hopes he will come back this evening: will → Hoffnung

Look at him, I will help him with his heavy bags. →

Oh no, the dog is going to bite (*beißen*) her. →

We are going to buy a present for mum on Saturday. →

AUFGABE 2 **Hier geht es um unbeeinflussbare Ereignisse, Hoffnungen, Vermutungen und spontane Entscheidungen. Setze die passende Zukunftsform ein.**

Ben: "I hope we ______ (not / to get) too much homework for today. What ______ (the weather / to be) like in the afternoon?"

Paul: "I think it ______ (to be) nice and sunny in the afternoon. If we do not get a lot of homework, we ______ (to have) time to play together."

Ben: "We can ask our teacher. I hope she ______ (not / to give) us too much homework."

AUFGABE 3 **Hier werden Verabredungen, Pläne und absehbare Ereignisse beschrieben. Setze die passende Zukunftsform ein.**

Mary: "______ (you / to come) to our party on Saturday? We ______ (to have) a barbecue *(Grillfest)*."

Sandra: "Yes, I ______ (to come). My mum ______ (to get) some veggie burgers."

Mary: "______ (you / to sleep) here?"

Sandra: "No, my mum ______ (to pick) me up after the party."

TESTEN

AUFGABE 4 **Setze *will*- oder *going to-future* ein.**

If I go to Edinburgh, I ______ (to visit) my aunt.

______ (you / to buy) a bike?

We ______ (to have) lasagne for dinner.

I think I ______ (to like) this work.

AUFGABE 5 **Füge die Elemente zu Sätzen zusammen und entscheide dich für die richtige Zukunftsform. Schreibe in dein Übungsheft.**

(Year 2030: You are a pilot) a pilot – to be – I
We hope – happy – she – to be – in Australia
to play football – on Sunday – you – ?
(You look tired:) not – we – to climb up – the hill
(Our plans for Saturday changed:) not – we – to climb up – the hill

AUFGABE 6 **Übersetze die Frage und gib eine verneinte Antwort.**

Wird sie den Test bestehen *(to pass)*? ______

______

Werde ich glücklich sein? ______

______

Wird Richard am Wochenende kommen? ______

______

Werdet ihr zusammen *(together)* spielen? ______

______

AUFGABE 7 **Wie sieht deine Zukunft aus? Bilde zu den Stichwörtern Sätze mit der passenden Zukunftsform. Schreibe in dein Übungsheft.**

Beispiel: Ein fester Plan für nächstes Jahr. → I'm going to learn a lot.

Ein fester Plan für nächsten Monat.
Eine Vorhersage über deinen zukünftigen Beruf.
Ein festes Vorhaben für nächste Woche.
Eine Vorhersage über das Wetter am nächsten Wochenende.
Eine Vorhersage über deinen zukünftigen Wohnort.

Klassenarbeit 2

45 Minuten

AUFGABE 8 **Unterstreiche die richtige Verbform.**

Look at the sky. It will snow / is going to snow any minute now.

I think it will rain / is going to rain tomorrow.

Sally can't go out tonight. She will do / is going to do her homework.

Are you going to the cinema? Wait a minute. I will go / am going to go with you.

My dad has made up his mind. He will stop / is going to stop smoking.

If you go by train next week, I will take / am going to take you to the station.

AUFGABE 9 **Was passiert als nächstes? Lies dir die folgenden Situationen durch und wähle dann das richtige Verb aus dem Wortspeicher um zu beschreiben, was als nächstes mit großer Wahrscheinlichkeit passieren wird. Verwende das *going to-future*.**

to fall down – to break – to walk into – to drop – to rain –
to crash into – to write

Penny is carrying a lot of books that are too heavy for her. She ________________ some of them.

There are lot of dark clouds in the sky. It ________________.

Jack isn't careful enough and there is a man standing right in front of him. He ________________ that man.

Dave is in his classroom and he has got some chalk. He ________________ something on the board.

Luke is driving far too quickly. Hopefully, he isn't ________________ into a tree.

Look, there are two boys ice skating, but the temperatures are above zero. The ice ________________.

Mrs Snyder's cat has climbed up her tree again. It's Kitty again at the top of tree. She ________________. Poor thing. Last time the firemen had to rescue her.

TESTEN

AUFGABE 10 ***Will-future*** **oder** ***going to-future*****: Wähle die richtige Verbform.**

Brian, I'm sure you _____ (to enjoy) your stay in Wales. Maybe the weather _____ (to be) fantastic.

There are hardly any clouds. So the sun _____ (to shine).

We bought a house in York last year. We _____ (to move) up north.

Do you think it _____ (to be) cold tomorrow?

Would you like to come to Angela's birthday party? – Well, I _____ (to think) about it.

Perhaps Sue _____ (to meet) him again one day.

I'm afraid Matthew can't come tonight. He _____ (to play) in an important football match tomorrow.

Kim _____ (to have) a proper breakfast before she goes hiking.

AUFGABE 11 **Korrigiere die folgenden Sätze und schreibe sie noch einmal richtig in dein Übungsheft.**

ACHTUNG FEHLER

It is wet when we arrive in the Lake District.
Pete looks for a job in London.
Be careful. It is raining and there are a lot of leaves on the ground. You are slipping.
Will loves travelling. He travels for a year.
Jane's birthday is on a Wednesday this year.
Wait a minute! I'm helping you.
If I don't go to bed early, I'm tired the next day.
Look at this kitchen table: butter, sugar, flour. Mum will make a cake.

AUFGABE 12 **Übersetze die folgenden Sätze ins Englische. Achte dabei auf die richtige Verwendung der Zukunft. Schreibe in dein Übungsheft.**

Ich bin nicht sicher, ob ich dieses Fahrrad kaufe.
Zoe hat Konzertkarten. Sie geht am Freitag ins Konzert.
Pam und Lucy haben fest vor, am Wochenende eine Party zu feiern.
Weihnachten ist dieses Jahr an einem Sonntag.
Setz dich. Ich schließe das Fenster.

5 Der Satz

5.1 Bejahte Aussagesätze

Präge dir die englische Satzstellung ein:

Subjekt + (Hilfsverb +) Vollverb + Ergänzungen

Subjekt	Hilfsverb	Vollverb	Ergänzungen
My brother		goes	to primary school.
We	were	drinking	tea.

Das *simple present* und das *simple past* werden **ohne Hilfsverb** gebildet.

She lives in London.
She learned English.

Mit Hilfsverb + Vollverb werden gebildet:

- ***will-future:*** *will* + Vollverb — He will be happy.
- ***going to-future:*** *to be* + *going to* + Vollverb — They are going to meet Ann.
- ***past progressive:*** *was/were* + Vollverb + *-ing*-Form — Sally was wearing a funny dress.
- ***present perfect:*** *to have* + *past participle* — Lucy has tidied her room.
- **Modalsätze:** Modalverb + Vollverb — We must study for the test. I can sing a song.

Aufgepasst: Die Satzstellung im Englischen unterscheidet sich vom Deutschen.

- Englisch:
Subjekt + Hilfsverb + **Vollverb + Objekt**
- Deutsch:
Subjekt + Hilfsverb + **Objekt + Vollverb**

I can repair the bike.
Aber: Ich kann das Fahrrad reparieren.
We must visit him.
Aber: Wir müssen ihn besuchen.

Konjunktionen (Bindewörter)

Konjunktionen verbinden Wörter und Satzteile miteinander. Es gibt

- **einfache** Verbindungen: *and, or, but, because, so (daher), when (als), although (obwohl),*
- **gepaarte** Verbindungen: *either ... or (entweder ... oder), neither ... nor (weder noch).*

We sat down because we were tired.
They were unhappy so they left.

You can either go to Greece or to Spain.
Tina neither likes oranges nor apples.

ÜBUNG 1 **Bilde aus Subjekt und Verb einen Satz. Achte auf die Zeitform und füge eine passende Satzergänzung aus dem Wortspeicher hinzu.**

a present – my clothes – the table – ~~a bottle of water~~ – a letter – the Prince of Wales – to the shop

simple past: Mrs Taylor – to drink

Mrs Taylor drank a bottle of water.

simple past: James – her – to give

simple present: can – he – write

past progressive: George and his brother – to go

present perfect: Richard – to paint

simple present: must – I – to change

going to-future: the Queen – to meet

WISSEN

Adverbialbestimmungen und Adverbien
Achte besonders auf die Stellung von Adverbialbestimmungen der Zeit, des Ortes sowie von Adverbien.

- Im Deutschen steht die Zeitangabe vor der Ortsangabe, im Englischen ist es umgekehrt: **Ort vor Zeit!**

  Ich war um 17 Uhr im Supermarkt.
  Aber: I was at the supermarket at five.

- **Adverbien der Häufigkeit** wie *always, ever, never, often, sometimes* stehen in der Regel **vor** dem Vollverb.

  Peter **sometimes** does the dishes.
  I have **never** seen such a thing.

- **Adverbien der Art und Weise** stehen normalerweise hinter dem Objekt.

  She answered the questions **nervously.**
  She laughed **happily.**

ÜBUNG 2 **Ordne die Satzteile zu ganzen Sätzen. Achte auf die Satzstellung. Schreibe in dein Übungsheft.**

simple present: I – to play CDs – often
simple past: in his room – he – sometimes – to listen to music – in the evenings
simple present: Tina – to visit – never – her grandmother
going to-future: on Sunday – my father – to play badminton – and I – in the park
simple past: in town – Sarah – on a fine day – to go shopping – last week
going to-future: in the kitchen – to cook dinner – we – at six o'clock
present perfect: to do – carefully – they – always – their homework

ÜBUNG 3 **Ergänze die folgenden Sätze. Höre dir dazu Track 8 auf der CD an.**

8

She bought a lot of clothes although ______.

Jim was unfair so ______.

I opened the window because ______.

Mrs Walker wanted to come but ______.

Rose likes to ski although ______.

Mrs Craig wanted her pupils to be quiet but ______.

The children are playing inside because ______.

The kitchen looks a mess so ______.

ÜBUNG 4 **Übersetze die Sätze.**

Meine Eltern kauften letztes Jahr ein Haus.

______

Fred lernt seit neun Jahren Spanisch.

______

Philipp und Greg kauften weder Blumen noch ein anderes Geschenk.

______

Jim räumt manchmal den Tisch ab *(to clear)*.

______

Ich kann morgen auf die Party gehen.

______

5.2 Verneinte Aussagesätze

Verneinte Aussagesätze werden wie bejahte Aussagesätze gebildet. Hinzu kommt der verneinende Zusatz *not*: **Subjekt + Hilfsverb + *not* + Vollverb + Ergänzungen**	I have not done my homework. I am not talking to you. They did not clean their rooms.
Es gibt verschiedene Hilfsverben: Die Formen von *to be, to have, to do* sowie die Modalverben *can, may* und *must.*	be → I am / was not going to India. have → I have not been to India. do → I do not / did not go to India. can → I cannot go to India.
Merke: must wird zu *need not / needn't* (↑ Kap. 2.3)!	must → I need not go to India.
Verneinte Zeitformen werden mit dem entsprechenden Hilfsverb + *not* + Vollverb gebildet:	
■ ***present progressive:*** *am / are / is* + not + Vollverb + *-ing*	They are not singing a song.
■ ***will-future:*** *will* + *not* + Vollverb	He will not be happy.
■ ***going to-future:*** *am / are / is* + *not* + *going to* + Vollverb	They are not going to meet their friends.
■ ***past progressive:*** *was / were* + *not* + Vollverb + *-ing*	Lisa was not wearing a hat.
■ ***present perfect:*** *have / has* + *not* + *past participle*	Tim has not tidied his room.
■ **Modalsätze:** Modalverb + *not* + Vollverb	I cannot go to school today. We must not go to the cinema at 10 p.m.
Aufgepasst: In Aussagesätzen im ***simple present*** benötigst du bei der Verneinung das Hilfsverb ***to do*** + *not* + Vollverb! Das verneinte ***simple past*** wird durch ***did*** + *not* + Vollverb angezeigt.	Frank speaks French. → Frank does not speak French. She wrote a letter. → She did not write a letter.
Achtung: Bei Negativwörtern wie *nobody, never* und *nothing* brauchst du kein zusätzliches *not* einsetzen.	Nobody came in. I have never been to the museum. I had nothing to do with it.

ÜBUNG 5 **Unterstreiche und kennzeichne in den folgenden bejahten Aussagesätzen alle Hilfsverben (Hv) und alle Vollverben (Vv).**

They can go to the doctor.

Hv Vv

He was sitting on the chair.

She went to bed early.

Christina has worked for two hours.

Lydia and Kim were having fun.

He wrote an e-mail.

Tina is eating a banana.

WISSEN

Die Kurzform der Verneinung
In der Schriftsprache verwendet man die Langform, in der gesprochenen Sprache meist die Kurzform der Hilfs- und Modalverben.

Aufgepasst: May not existiert nur in der Langform!

do / does not → don't / doesn't
did not → didn't
was / were not → wasn't / weren't
have / has not → haven't / hasn't
had not → hadn't
will not → won't
cannot → can't
could not → couldn't
must not → mustn't

ÜBUNG 6 **Verneine nun die Sätze aus Übung 5. Schreibe jeweils Kurz- und Langform.**

ÜBEN

ÜBUNG 7 **Bilde vollständige verneinte Sätze mit der angegebenen Zeit.**

simple present: we – to go – to school

We don't go to school.

simple past: they – to listen – to music

simple past: Liz – to work – in the garden

simple present: Larry – to buy – a present

simple past: we – to watch – TV

simple past: I – to clean – the windows

simple present: she – to read – the book

simple present: they – to go – to the museum

ÜBUNG 8 **Übersetze die folgenden Sätze. Schreibe in dein Übungsheft.**

Tino ging gestern nicht nach Hause.
Niemand aß den Kuchen.
Walter und Ian nahmen nicht den Bus *(to take, past progressive).*
Rita wird sich nicht mit Tina treffen *(going to-future).*
Sie haben nie ein Buch gelesen.
Janice half ihrer Mutter nicht.

ÜBEN

ÜBUNG 9 **Bilde aus den folgenden Satzteilen verneinte Sätze.**

simple present: can – mum – to cook

simple past: to jump – on the chair – I

present perfect: to read – she – for two weeks – a book

simple present: Charly – soon – must – go home *(Vorsicht)*

will-future: it – today – rain

going to-future: now – to sing – Freddy – for us

simple past: nobody – to sing – a song

present perfect: I – to school – to go – yet

simple present: may – to know – they – it

present perfect: to be – they – never – to France

will-future: they – to come

5.3 Bedingungssätze

Die Bildung von Bedingungssätzen

Bedingungssätze *(conditional sentences,* auch: *if-clauses)* beinhalten
- eine **Bedingung** und
- eine daraus abgeleitete **Folge**.

If you ring the bell, I will open the door.
If I pass the exam, I will be happy.
If you work too much, you will get tired.

Bedingungssätze bestehen aus einem *if*-Satz (Bedingung) + Hauptsatz (Folge). Die Reihenfolge dieser beiden Satzteile ist austauschbar.

If Tom runs, he will catch the bus.
Tom will catch the bus if he runs.

Achtung: Steht der *if*-Satz an zweiter Stelle, entfällt das Komma!

Achte auf die **Zeiten** in den beiden Satzteilen:
- Der *if*-Satz steht im ***simple present***,
- der Hauptsatz wird mit dem ***will-future*** gebildet.

If Aunt Helen visits us, we will show her the house.
If Tim gets up early, he will catch the 9:30 train.

Der Unterschied zwischen *if* und *when*

If und ***when*** bedeuten beide *wenn*. Sie werden jedoch unterschiedlich gebraucht.

If kannst du auch mit *falls* übersetzen. Es handelt sich um eine **Bedingung,** die etwas zur Folge hat.

If Jane comes to the party, we will have fun. → Wenn / Falls Jane auf die Party kommt, dann werden wir Spaß haben (wenn sie nicht kommt, dann nicht).

Bei ***when*** ist ein **Zeitpunkt** gemeint, zu dem etwas geschehen wird. Anstatt *wenn* kann man auch *sobald* sagen.

When Jane comes to the party, we will start the game. → Wenn / Sobald Jane auf die Party kommt, fangen wir mit dem Spiel an (Jane hat gesagt, dass sie kommt, aber sie ist noch nicht da).

When-Sätze werden wie *if*-Sätze gebildet.

If mum arrives earlier, we will start cooking sooner.
When mum arrives, we will start cooking.

ÜBUNG 10 **Füge die passende Verbform ein.**

If Kim ______ (to visit) Tom, she ______ (to have) a good time.

If our team ______ (to win) the match, we ______ (to have) a big party.

If it ______ (to rain), Tim and Gina ______ (to go) by bus.

Mr Jones ______ (to catch) the 7:15 train if he ______ (to leave) immediately *(sofort)*.

If they ______ (to visit) Aunt Jill, they ______ (to see) the picture.

My parents ______ (to sell) our old car when they ______ (to buy) a new one.

If Simon ______ (to write) her an e-mail, Tina ______ (to be) happy.

If you ______ (to eat) too much chocolate, you ______ (to feel) bad.

WISSEN

Die Verneinung von Bedingungssätzen

- verneinter *if*-Satz: If it **doesn't** rain, we will go to the park.
  If you **aren't** honest *(ehrlich)*, you will get problems.
- verneinter Hauptsatz: If you drink coffee in the evening, you **will not / won't** sleep.
  If John forgets his homework, he **will not / won't** get a good mark.
- beide Satzteile verneint: If she **doesn't** come, she **will not / won't** see the show.
  If you **don't** eat the cake, you **will not / won't** get fat.

ÜBUNG 11 **Bilde vollständige Bedingungssätze. Verbinde die *if*-Satzteile mit den Hauptsatzteilen. Schreibe die Sätze in dein Übungsheft.**

if-Satz	Hauptsatz
I (to tell) you the truth	we (to get) good marks
you (not – to call) her	you (to be) shocked
Susan (to stay) longer	he (not – pass) the exams
you (to go) to bed early	she (to be) angry
we (to work) hard	she (to miss) the bus
he (not – to do) his homework	you (not – to be) tired the next morning

ÜBUNG 12 **Fülle die Lücken mit den richtigen Zeitformen und entscheide, ob du *when* oder *if* einsetzen musst.**

Mum ___ (to be) there ___ (Bedingung) you ___ (to arrive) at 7 o'clock.

___ (Zeitpunkt) we ___ (to start) eating, you ___ (not – to be) hungry anymore.

Sally ___ (to read) the book ___ (Zeitpunkt) she ___ (to get) it.

Henry ___ (to win) the match ___ (Bedingung) Sandy ___ (not – to play) well.

___ (Zeitpunkt) she ___ (to arrive) at the hotel, she ___ (to meet) him.

___ (Bedingung) you ___ (to make) too many mistakes, you ___ (not – to pass) the exam.

ÜBUNG 13 **Übersetze die Sätze ins Englische: *if* oder *when*?**

Ich werde nach Hause gehen, wenn (sobald) es dunkel wird.

___

Meine Mutter wird böse sein, wenn (falls) ich nicht komme.

___

Mr Jordan wird die Hunde füttern, wenn (sobald) wir ihn bitten *(to ask)*.

___

Simon wird nicht einkaufen gehen, wenn (falls) ihn seine Mutter nicht bittet.

___

Wenn (sobald / falls) Tina die Nachricht *(message)* liest, wird sie unglücklich sein.

___

5.4 Relativsätze

Die Bildung von Relativsätzen

Ein **Relativsatz *(relative clause)*** erweitert einen Satz, indem er Personen, Dinge oder Tiere näher beschreibt.

This is the man	who bought the car.
↓	↓
Hauptsatz	Relativsatz

Relativsätze werden durch **Relativpronomen** eingeleitet:

- ***who*** und ***that*** beziehen sich auf Personen; die Objektform lautet ***whom***,
- ***which*** und ***that*** beziehen sich auf Dinge oder Tiere,
- ***whose*** zeigt eine Zugehörigkeit oder ein Besitzverhältnis an („wessen?“).

A doctor is a person **who** can help people.

This is the book, **which** you gave me.

The man **whose** daughter won the competition is a teacher.

Die Verwendung von Relativsätzen

Ein **Relativsatz *(relative clause)*** bestimmt das Bezugswort näher. Einen Relativsatz, der für das Verständnis des gesamten Satzes notwendig ist, nennt man einen **notwendigen Relativsatz *(defining relative clause)*.**
Bei Personen steht *who / that*, bei Dingen und Tieren *which / that*.

This is the girl **who / that** lives next door.
Robert loves books **which / that** are exciting.

Ohne den Relativsatz wäre die Aussage des Hauptsatzes nicht vollständig: Es wäre nicht klar, wer oder was genau gemeint ist.

Merke: Es steht kein Komma vor dem Relativsatz!

Relativsätze mit und ohne Relativpronomen

Wird ein Relativpronomen in einem notwendigen Relativsatz als **Subjekt** („wer oder was?“) verwendet, darf es **nicht weggelassen** werden!

My grandma is an old lady **who** always wears a skirt.
(Wer trägt immer Röcke? → the old lady)

Wird ein Relativpronomen in einem notwendigen Relativsatz als **Objekt** („wen oder was?") verwendet, **kann** es **weggelassen** werden.

My grandma is an old lady **who** I like very much.
(Wen mag ich? → the old lady)

Merke: Ein notwendiger Relativsatz ohne Relativpronomen heißt *contact clause*.

→ My grandma is an old lady I like very much.

Zur Probe, ob du das Relativpronomen weglassen kannst, musst du die **Subjekt- oder Objektfrage** stellen:

- „wer oder was?" → Subjekt → das Relativpronomen muss stehen,

Gina is a person who eats a lot.
(„Wer isst viel?")
→ kein Weglassen von who möglich!

- „wen oder was?"/ „wem?" → Objekt → das Relativpronomen kann entfallen.

Aber:
Gina is a person who you can trust.
(„Wem kannst du vertrauen?")
→ Weglassen von who ist möglich:
Gina is a person you can trust.

Achtung: In nicht notwendigen Relativsätzen darf *who* oder *which* **nicht** weggelassen werden!

My brother, **who** could help me, is on holiday.
We spent our holidays in London, **which** is a big city.

Präpositionen im notwendigen Relativsatz

In einem notwendigen Relativsatz kann eine Präposition stehen

- vor dem Relativpronomen *who* oder *which*,
- am Ende des Satzes, wenn das Relativpronomen *that* ist,
- am Ende des Satzes in einem *contact clause*.

This is the pen **with which** I write at school.
This is the pen **that** I write at school **with.**

This is the pen I write at school with.

Merke: Vor *that* steht niemals eine Präposition.

Ein Relativsatz kann durch *where* oder *when* eingeleitet werden, wenn das Bezugswort einen Ort oder einen Zeitpunkt angibt.

This is the house **in which** (= where) I live.
I give you the time **at which** (= when) we must leave.

ÜBUNG 14 **Relativpronomen leiten einen Relativsatz ein. Welche Relativpronomen kennst du und auf wen oder was beziehen sie sich?**

___ h ___ :

P ___

w ___ ___ ___ ___ :

D ___ oder T ___

t ___ ___ ___ :

P ___ , D ___ , T ___

w ___ o ___ ___ :

zeigt eine Z ___ an

ÜBUNG 15 **Unterstreiche den Relativsatz und kreise das Relativpronomen ein.**

This is the man who bought the car.

A Smart is a car which is small.

He is the boy who took the CD.

People who drive too fast are stupid.

These are the books that are cheap.

Ted, who found the money, is a young man.

ÜBEN

ÜBUNG 16 **Setze das fehlende Relativpronomen ein.**

This is the old lady whose garden I like.

Frederic is a boy _____ can sing and play the guitar.

Jason's mother is a nurse _____ works at General Hospital.

They showed a film _____ was brilliant.

This is Margret _____ aunt works in the bakery.

This is my friend Ron _____ bought a blue bike.

Mr Harold is the neighbour _____ dogs are always barking (*bellen*).

Mrs Richard is the teacher _____ went bungee jumping last year.

ÜBUNG 17 **Beschreibe die folgenden Personen und Dinge näher. Verwende die angegebenen Satzteile, indem du das richtige Relativpronomen einsetzt.**

to be very famous

to work with children

to look like a beetle (Käfer)

~~to help people~~

to look after sheep

to colour your lips

to work in a restaurant

A nurse is a person who helps people.

A sheperd (*Schäfer*) is a person _____

A teacher is a person _____

A VW Beetle is a car _____

A lipstick is like a pen _____

Brad Pitt is an actor _____

A waiter is someone _____

ÜBUNG 18 **Gib an, ob es sich bei dem Relativpronomen um ein Subjekt oder Objekt handelt und ob das Relativpronomen weggelassen werden kann!**

1. Mr Brown is the police officer who asked the questions.
   Frage: **Wer** stellte die Fragen? → who (the police officer)

   ☐ *Who* wird als Subjekt gebraucht und kann nicht weggelassen werden.

   ☐ *Who* wird als Objekt gebraucht und kann weggelassen werden.

   Der Satz lautet dann:

2. Take the cheese that I bought yesterday.
   Frage: **Wen oder was** kaufte ich? → that (the cheese)

   ☐ *That* wird als Subjekt gebraucht und kann nicht weggelassen werden.

   ☐ *That* wird als Objekt gebraucht und kann weggelassen werden.

   Der Satz lautet dann:

ÜBUNG 19 **Wird das Relativpronomen in den folgenden Sätzen als Objekt oder als Subjekt gebraucht? Wenn es als Objekt verwendet wird, kann man es weglassen – streiche es in diesem Fall durch.**

This is the key which I was looking for.

Teresa helped grandma who was in hospital.

Mrs Rose is the teacher who Francis had in biology.

Take the shirt which is in the washing machine.

Take the cup which you like most.

Where is the CD that I got for my birthday?

This is the watch which is broken.

Luke likes the book which he has just read.

Anna loves the boy who sits next to her in class.

My father is a man who collects stamps.

ÜBUNG 20 Finde den passenden Relativsatz. Wenn das Relativpronomen Objekt des Relativsatzes ist, lasse es weg.

young and old people like

are happy

you can trust *(vertrauen)*

works for a big company

wrote a lot of novels

Linda found last week

was lying on the street

I was using for my letter

Jane Austen is a British author ...

Volleyball is a team sport ...

I like people ...

Justin is a boy ...

It's Jim's box ...

Marion loves a man ...

Where is the pen ...

The car hit the tree ...

ÜBUNG 21 **Höre dir Track 9 auf der CD an und ergänze die Sätze.**

9

Can you see ______ is in front of the shop?

This is ______ helps me with my homework.

This is ______ I couldn't do.

Is this ______ CDs you like?

Have you got ______ is sharp enough for the bread?

Peter is ______ lives in Peru.

These are ______ daughter sings in a famous choir.

They stole ______ was in her jacket.

Is this ______ bark is worse than its bite?

Look at ______ are dancing over there!

ÜBUNG 22 **Verbinde jeweils einen Satz aus der linken und rechten Spalte zu einem Hauptsatz und einem Relativsatz.**

Gina's mother works for a company.	She is interested in art.
Queen Elizabeth doesn't have to pay the rent *(Miete)*.	He is sitting at the table next to us.
This is the old CD.	It was in my bag.
The old man is blind.	She lives in Buckingham Palace.
Babette is an old friend.	The company produces computers.

ÜBEN

Klassenarbeit 1

45 Minuten

AUFGABE 1 **Bejahte und verneinte Aussagesätze: Ordne die einzelnen Satzteile in der richtigen Reihenfolge. Schreibe die Sätze in dein Übungsheft.**

I / for four years / lived / in Berlin / have.
like / did / Dana / not / the show.
start / Francis / the race / cannot.
was / not / I / of the test / afraid.
wash / is / going to / Simon / the car.
was / she / cleaning / her bike / not.

AUFGABE 2 **Setze das fehlende Bindewort ein.**

He went to bed ______ (weil) he was tired.

You can ______ (entweder) have coffee ______ (oder) tea.

Tom doesn't talk to Pam ______ (obwohl) he likes her.

John didn't win the prize ______ (aber) the audience *(Publikum)* loved him.

This is ______ (weder) my dog ______ (noch) his dog.

AUFGABE 3 **Falsche Satzstellung! Verbessere jeweils den ganzen Satz und schreibe ihn richtig in dein Übungsheft.**

ACHTUNG FEHLER

Always we go on Saturday evenings to the cinema.
Tim forgets never his keys.
My mother plays in the evening sometimes the piano.
We go skiing in winter often.

AUFGABE 4 **Bilde verneinte Aussagesätze. Achte auf die richtige Zeit und schreibe Lang- und Kurzform. Schreibe die Sätze in dein Übungsheft.**

to clean his bike / Frank *(simple past)*
to sit in the bar / she *(past progressive)*
to come / Tom *(going to-future)*
to see the bird / Betty *(present perfect)*
to listen to music / they *(simple past)*
to be a film star / I *(will-future)*
to buy a skirt / Sarah *(present perfect)*
to catch the thieves / the police *(simple past)*

AUFGABE 5 **Bedingungssätze bestehen aus einem Hauptsatz und einem *if*-Satz. Setze die fehlenden Verben in der richtigen Zeit ein.**

Kevin ______ (to be) a good student if he ______ (to learn) more.

The cat ______ (to fall) down if it ______ (to stop / not).

If we ______ (to start) now, we ______ (to finish) at 12 o'clock.

If Sue ______ (to walk) faster, she ______ (to get / not) wet.

If you ______ (to wait) for me, I ______ (to help) you.

AUFGABE 6 **Setze die passenden Relativpronomen ein.**

Is this your bike ______ is standing in front of the tree?

Give me the book ______ is on the shelf.

Can you show me the lady ______ bag this is?

This is my brother ______ works at the cinema.

Mrs Johnson is the lady ______ son lives in Canada.

Are you the boy ______ lives next door?

AUFGABE 7 **Wann kannst du das Relativpronomen weglassen? Trage es nur in den Sätzen ein, wo es nicht fehlen darf.**

Look at the girl ______ is next to Peter.

Mum baked a cake ______ you will like a lot.

Take the plate ______ is clean.

This is the friend ______ can juggle (*jonglieren*).

Carina is reading the book ______ Tim was talking about.

Did you know the man ______ asked for some money?

AUFGABE 8 **Übersetze die folgenden Sätze und schreibe sie in dein Übungsheft.**

Ruth und Kim sprachen gestern nicht mit mir.
Wenn du das Fahrrad reparierst, koche ich für dich.
Gina ist das Mädchen, das Basketball spielt.

Klassenarbeit 2

45 Minuten

AUFGABE 9 **Ergänze die folgende Tabelle, indem du entweder die richtige Zeitform einsetzt oder einen Satz mit den Satzteilen bildest.**

Zeitform	Satz
	She often goes to school by bike.
simple past: Alan / to write letters / yesterday	
present perfect: the children / to eat ice cream	
	I am in a hurry.
past progressive: Clive / to play tennis	
	Maybe her friends will come next week.
	Mum has just come upstairs.
going to-future: we / to visit / Aunt Beth	

AUFGABE 10 **In den folgenden Sätzen ist etwas mit der Satzstellung durcheinander geraten. Unterstreiche den Fehler und schreibe dann den Satz richtig.**

ACHTUNG FEHLER

We will meet at seven o'clock in front of the cinema.

The Millers go usually to France during their summer holidays.

Sue has been to London never.

Mary looked angrily at her dog.

At five o'clock we can meet on Friday.

AUFGABE 11 **Beende die folgenden Sätze. Die Konjunktion wird dir dabei behilflich sein.**

terrible storm – to go skiing – to swim really well – to be really expensive – to play football

I often go swimming but I never ______.

It was snowing yesterday so we never ______.

I have just bought those jeans although they never ______.

We had to go inside because there was never ______.

Joe started to swim when he was five so never ______.

AUFGABE 12 **Ergänze die folgenden Sätze mit dem richtigen Relativpronomen. Es gibt mehrere Lösungen.**

I like dogs ______ don't bark or bite.

I don't like people ______ talk all the time.

I don't like films ______ are about monsters.

I like books ______ are about wizards and fairies.

I like friends ______ don't tell lies.

AUFGABE 13 **Vervollständige die Sätze, indem du den Satzteil in der Klammer ins Englische übersetzt. Achte auf die Satzstellung.**

Tim gave Jane (gestern einige seiner alten CDs) ______.

Judy is waiting (vor dem alten Haus auf Veronica) ______.

Rick has just written (einige Emails an seine Freunde) ______.

I'm looking (in meinem Zimmer nach meinem Handy) ______.

I (suche oft nach meinem Stift) ______.

Klassenarbeit 3

45 Minuten

AUFGABE 14 **Fülle die Lücken mit *if* oder *when*.**

Is it okay ______ I open the window? ______ it is too cold, I'll close it at once.

______ we get home, we'll have tea. I have already made the sandwiches.

Ben, you must phone us ______ you arrive in Liverpool.

I'll get you something to eat ______ you are hungry.

My parents will pick us up from Kate's house ______ we phone.

______ you study for the next class test, you will get a good mark.

AUFGABE 15 **Verbessere die Fehler in den folgenden Bedingungssätzen.** ACHTUNG FEHLER

If you wait a minute, I go with you.

______

It will be quicker if you will go by train.

______

We will go swimming if the weather will be fine.

______

When I go to bed after 10 o'clock, I will oversleep.

______

AUFGABE 16 **Was wirst du in den folgenden Situationen machen? Ergänze die Bedingungssätze mit deinen eigenen Ideen.**

If I get a good mark in my English test, ______.

If I win the first prize in a competition, ______.

If I find a purse in the street, ______.

If I have an accident with my bike, ______.

If I'm hungry, ______.

If I'm too late for school, ______.

AUFGABE 17 **Setze die fehlenden Relativpronomen ein. Manchmal sind verschiedene Relativpronomen richtig.**

This must be the actor ______ Ben always talks about.

This is the bird ______ has a broken wing.

I don't like the shoes ______ Victoria is wearing.

I was angry with my friend ______ sister was rude to me.

There is the school ______ I went to for four years.

Is this the part of the palace ______ burnt down last year?

AUFGABE 18 **Bilde einen Satz aus den jeweils zwei Sätzen. Wähle das richtige Relativpronomen, benutze kein Relativpronomen in *contact clauses*. Achte auf die richtige Satzstellung.**

That's the disco. Robert met Sarah there.

This is the snack bar. It is famous for its crisps.

We saw the man. He lives in a huge house just across the road.

This is my uncle. His name is Billy.

Tim is a friend. I can trust him.

AUFGABE 19 **Übersetze die folgenden Sätze. Schreibe in dein Übungsheft.**

Falls es heftig schneit, wird der Direktor die Schule für zwei Tage schließen.
Sobald die Schule aus ist, laufen die meisten Kinder zur Bushaltestelle.
Fiona kennt nicht das Haus, in dem ihre Freundin wohnt.
Vor zwei Jahren haben wir unsere Ferien in Italien verbracht.
Gestern traf ich Sally gegen 3 Uhr in der Stadt.

6 Fragen

6.1 *Simple past* und *past progressive*

Die Bildung von Fragen im *simple past*

In der einfachen Vergangenheit *(simple past)* gibt es zwei Arten, eine Frage zu bilden:

- Fragen mit dem **Vollverb *to be***: (Fragewort +) *was / were* + Subjekt
- Fragen mit **anderen Vollverben**: (Fragewort +) *did* + Subjekt + Vollverb

Were you ill?
How was the show?
Did she eat in the kitchen?
What did you do yesterday?

Verneinte Fragen werden mit *was / were* + *not* oder *did* + *not* gebildet.

Wasn't she here yesterday?
Didn't you write me a letter?

Die Bildung von Fragen im *past progressive*

In der Verlaufsform der Vergangenheit *(past progressive)* wird eine Frage nur mit *was / were* gebildet:

- (Fragewort) + *was / were* + Subjekt + Vollverb
- Verneinte Fragen werden mit *was / were* + *not* gebildet.

Were they painting the room?
Was she having fun?
Where was Anna waiting?
Who was watching the movie?
Weren't you cleaning the kitchen?

Frageformen

Es gibt verschiedene Frageformen:

- Eine **Entscheidungsfrage** ist eine Frage ohne Fragewort. Es wird entweder „ja" oder „nein" erwartet.
  Als Antwort gibst du eine Kurzantwort *(short answer)* (↑ S. 103).

Were you hungry? – Yes, I was.
Weren't you tired yesterday? – No, I wasn't.
Was he walking alone? – Yes, he was.

- Eine **Ergänzungsfrage** ist eine Frage mit einem Fragewort. Sie fragt nach Informationen, die über „ja" und „nein" hinausgehen.
  Bei der Antwort ist keine Kurzantwort möglich.

Who was here? – Simon was here and brought some flowers.
What did you do? – I went to the shop.
Why was he running so fast? – He was late for school.

Die wichtigsten **Fragewörter** sind:

what – was	What were you doing?
where – wo / wohin	Where is Patrick?
when – wann	When did John leave the house?
who – wer / wen	Who is coming in?
why – warum	Why were they angry?
whose – wessen	Whose car is it?
how – wie	How many bottles are left?

Ergänzungsfragen

Ergänzungsfragen fragen nach dem Subjekt oder nach anderen Satzteilen.
Bei Fragen nach dem **Subjekt** *(who?)* steht

- das Fragewort anstelle des Subjekts,
- in verneinten Fragen *does / did.*

Who visited grandma?
(„wer?" – der Enkel besuchte sie)
Who didn't pass the exam?
(„wer?" – John fiel durch die Prüfung)

Bei Fragen nach anderen **Satzteilen**

- ist die Satzstellung die gleiche wie im *simple present* (Fragewort + Hilfsverb + Subjekt + Vollverb),
- steht *did* und *didn't* (im *simple present: do / does* und *don't / doesn't*).

What did you put on the table?
When did you leave school?
Where did he go? (Where does he go?)
Why didn't you go home?
(Why don't you go home?)

Question tags

Question tags sind **Frageanhängsel**, die mit *oder* oder *nicht wahr* übersetzt werden können.

You passed the exam, didn't you? – Du hast die Prüfung bestanden, nicht wahr?

- Frage mit ***to be:*** Im Frageanhängsel wird die entsprechende Form von *to be* wiederholt.

The pizza was good, wasn't it?
The pizza wasn't good, was it?

- Frage mit einem **anderen Vollverb**: Im Frageanhängsel wird *did* benötigt.

Frank worked hard, didn't he?
Frank didn't work hard, did he?

Merke: Ein bejahter Satz erhält ein verneintes Frageanhängsel, ein verneinter Satz erhält ein bejahtes Frageanhängsel!

ÜBUNG 1 **Hier sind sieben Fragewörter versteckt. Schreibe sie heraus und übersetze sie.**

Z	W	B	Y	J	N	W	B
W	H	O	Q	Q	G	H	V
V	E	A	E	R	F	Y	Z
X	R	S	Z	G	L	H	I
H	E	W	H	O	S	E	Z
O	U	R	R	A	O	C	C
W	H	E	N	W	B	H	J
U	M	R	H	W	H	A	T

ÜBUNG 2 **Wandle die Fragen vom *simple present* in das *simple past* um. Schreibe die Sätze in dein Übungsheft.**

Where are you?
Who goes to school?
How are they?
Why do you like potatoes?
Whose jeans are these?
When does the shop open?
What books do you like?
Who is your favourite actor?

ÜBUNG 3 **Setze die einzelnen Sätze in die Frageform und achte auf die richtige Zeit.**

Mum bought a book.
He was going to school.
They were afraid of the test.
You studied for the test.

ÜBUNG 4 **Ersetze in folgenden Ergänzungsfragen die roten Satzteile mit einem Fragewort und formuliere die ganze Frage.**

John slept until noon. — Who slept until noon?
Jonathan went to Hamburg.
Jimmy sat on the chair.
He played football on Saturday.
This was Jimmy's bike.

WISSEN

Fehlerquelle: *was / were* oder *did?*
Achte genau darauf, ob im Ausagesatz
- *was / were* steht: Dann bildest du auch die Frage mit *was / were*.
- ein Vollverb steht: Dann musst du die Frage mit *did* bilden.

Aufgepasst: Das *simple past* wird bereits durch das *did* ausgedrückt, deshalb folgt das Vollverb **immer** in der Grundform!

He was happy. → Was he happy?
You were at home. → Were you at home?
You cleaned the door. → Did you clean the door?
She looked at you. → Did she look at you?

ÜBUNG 5 **Achte auf die Satzfragmente und bilde Entscheidungsfragen im *simple past*. Schreibe in dein Übungsheft.**

Beispiel: to be hungry – they → Were they hungry?

to sit in the park – she
to help grandma – you
to write an e-mail – not – he
to be hungry – you
to listen to a CD – they
to be alone – he
to be old – they
to go skating – you
to be ready – they
to fly to Rome – not – he

ÜBUNG 6 **Die folgenden Sätze enthalten viele Informationen. Formuliere verschiedene Fragen nach den einzelnen Satzteilen.**

1. Frank visited his aunt in Birmingham.

Who
What
Who
Where

ÜBEN

2. Sandra and Jenny saw an old lady in the park who looked very sad.

Who

What

What / Who

Where

Who

How

ÜBUNG 7 **Wandle die folgenden Satzfragmente in eine *simple past*-Frage und danach in eine *past progressive*-Frage um. Schreibe in dein Übungsheft.**

Beispiel: to watch TV – she → Did she watch TV? Was she watching TV?

to take pictures – you
to play volleyball – not – they
to go to the concert – he
to have fun – you
to buy a present – we
to write an essay – not – Tim

WISSEN +

Kurzantworten

Bei Entscheidungsfragen genügt es nicht, nur *yes* oder *no* zu sagen. Man braucht immer eine **Kurzantwort** *(short answer)*.

Steht in der Frage *was / were*, wird auch mit ***was / were*** geantwortet.

Was she ill? – Yes, she was.
Were they on holiday? – No, they were not / weren't.

Steht in der Frage *did* + Vollverb, wird auch mit ***did*** geantwortet.

Did they go to Spain? – Yes, they did.
Did you leave a message? – No, I didn't.

ÜBUNG 8 **Beantworte die Fragen mit einer Kurzantwort. Antworte jeweils mit „ja" und mit „nein". Schreibe die Antworten in dein Übungsheft.**

Did he buy the green shirt?
Did they play basketball?
Were you at the party?
Was she having fun all day long?
Was he sad?
Was the cat sitting next to us?

WISSEN

Question tags **(Frageanhängsel)**
Bei den *question tags* gelten die Regeln der Kurzantworten (↑ S. 103):
was / were → *wasn't / weren't*
andere Vollverben → *did!*

Merke: Positive Aussage → negatives Frageanhängsel,
negative Aussage → positives Frageanhängsel!

You were at the party, weren't you?
He played the guitar, didn't he?
She wasn't at school, was she?
She didn't call, did she?

ÜBUNG 9 **Ergänze die richtigen *question tags*.**

They weren't sitting in the kitchen, ______ ?

It rained in the afternoon, ______ ?

She didn't clean the room, ______ ?

Georgia wasn't in the hospital, ______ ?

They talked to Harry, ______ ?

ÜBUNG 10 **Höre dir Track 10 auf der CD an und ergänze das fehlende Fragewort.**

10

______ bought the shoes?

______ did Jane come home?

______ long has Gwen been living in Wales?

______ are you late again?

______ can I put my coat?

______ often has Robert phoned so far?

______ are you going to invite to your party?

ÜBEN

WISSEN ✚

some **und** ***any***	
Some wird in **bejahten Aussagesätzen** verwendet sowie in **höflichen Fragen, Vorschlägen** und **Antworten** benutzt; vor allem dann, wenn der Sprecher eine positive Antwort erwartet.	I bought some apples. Would you like to have some biscuits? – Yes, of course.
Any wird in **verneinten Aussagesätzen** und in **Fragen** verwendet. Im bejahten Aussagesatz bedeutet *any* jeder / jedes Beliebige.	She couldn't buy any apples. Have you got any problems? You can read any book you like.
Diese Regeln gelten auch für zusammengesetzte Formen mit *some* und *any*.	somebody, someone, something, somewhere anybody, anyone, anything, anywhere

ÜBUNG 11 **Vervollständige die Sätze mit *some* oder *any* und dem passenden Gegenstand.**

presents books fun milk meat some / any

I love to read. Have you got ______ ?

Tina is vegetarian. She doesn't like ______ .

Here is your tea. But I'm sorry, I haven't got ______ .

Let's have a party. I want to have ______ .

Soon it's Christmas. Have you already bought ______ ?

ÜBUNG 12 **Setze die passende Form von *some*, *any* oder einer Zusammensetzung ein.**

Verena wants to buy ______ apples. – He has lost his keys ______ . – Can ______ help me? – Are there ______ eggs left? – She hasn't got ______ to say. – I am wearing ______ new. – It was dark. I didn't see ______ . – Let's make ______ sandwiches. – Where are my keys? I can't find them ______ .

6.2 *Present perfect*

Frageformen

Beim einfachen Perfekt *(present perfect)* gibt es wie beim *simple past* verschiedene Frageformen (↑ Kap. 6.1):	
■ **Entscheidungsfragen** *(ja / nein)* und	Have you heard the news? – Yes, I have. / No, I haven't. Have you been to Ireland? – Yes, I have. / No, I haven't.
■ **Ergänzungsfragen** (weitere Informationen).	Where have you been? – I have been to Switzerland. What have you learned today? – We have learned some new words.

Die Bildung von Fragen im *present perfect*

Beim *present perfect* werden die Fragen immer mit *to have* gebildet: (Fragewort +) *have / has* + Subjekt + *past participle*	Have you ever been to Iceland? Where have you learned English?
Die **Kurzantworten** werden beim *present perfect* immer mit dem Hilfsverb ***to have*** gebildet.	Have you seen my purse? – Yes, I have. / No, I haven't. Hasn't he read the newspaper? – Yes, he has. / No, he hasn't.
Auch die **Frageanhängsel** werden mit *have / has* gebildet. *Merke:* Auch hier erfordert eine positive Aussage ein negatives Frageanhängsel und eine negative Aussage ein positives Frageanhängsel!	You have read this book, haven't you? We haven't got any money, have we?
Aufgepasst: Die Zeitangaben *already – schon* (im bejahten Satz) und *just – gerade eben* stehen in der Frage nach dem Subjekt und vor dem *past participle*. *Yet – schon* (im verneinten Satz) und *so far – bis jetzt, bisher* dagegen stehen am Ende des Satzes!	Have you already seen the new horror film? Has he just turned off the light? Where have you been so far? Haven't you done the washing-up yet?

ÜBUNG 13 **Setze das passende Fragewort ein.**

… has Kim been so far? … has helped Jim since April?

… have you been to Paris? … car have they stolen?

ÜBUNG 14 **Die folgenden Sätze sind nicht vollständig. Frage nach dem fehlenden Satzteil und benutze das *present perfect*.**
Beispiel: They have learned … since May. → What have they learned since May?

… has been to Russia. → ?

Simon has left his … at school. → ?

Mr Finn has been in … for five months. → ?

John and Steve have slept too long because … . → ?

… has not called yet. → ?

ÜBUNG 15 **Formuliere Fragen aus den Satzbausteinen.**

travelled / he / has / where / so far
just / Betty / what / has / read
Spanish / Richard / learned / has / for a long time
you / listened / have / yet / to the CD
have / I / seen / haven't I / you

ÜBUNG 16 **Übersetze. Schreibe die Lösungen in dein Übungsheft.**

Warst du schon in Paris?
Du hast die Küche nicht geputzt, oder *(question tag)*?
David, hast du Clare gesehen?
Wo hat Fred bisher gearbeitet?
Mr Keller ist nicht nach Japan geflogen, oder doch *(question tag)*?
Hat Vater schon angerufen?

Klassenarbeit 1

45 Minuten

AUFGABE 1 **Setze das passende Fragewort ein. Schreibe in Klammern, um welche Zeitform es sich handelt: *simple past, past progressive* oder *present perfect*.**

Where have they been since July? (present perfect)
did you watch on TV last night?
called the police?
was Tina painting the room?
long did you stay in Spain?

AUFGABE 2 **Wandle die Frage in die angegebene Zeitform um.**

Where are you? *(simple past)*

Does Kim sit next to you? *(past progressive)*

Where do you work? *(present perfect)*

Is Mum crying? *(past progressive)*

When must they leave the party? *(simple past)*

AUFGABE 3 **Frage nach den roten Satzteilen. Schreibe die Fragen in dein Übungsheft.**

They were having fun at the party.
Steve sat on the chair.
They watched TV.
Jane wrote the e-mail yesterday.
Grandpa was unhappy because he lost the game.
Harry's bike was dirty.
Gina was playing a computer game.

AUFGABE 4 **Formuliere die passende Entscheidungsfrage und gib bei „+“ eine positive und bei „–“ eine negative Kurzantwort.**

Beispiel: to rain – it – *past progressive* (–) → Was it raining? – No, it wasn't.

to fly to Los Angeles – Jack → *simple past* (+)
to live in London – you → *present perfect* (–)
to sell a car – he → *past progressive* (+)
to call the police – the old lady → *simple past* (–)
to read a lot of books – he → *present perfect* (–)

AUFGABE 5 **Bilde aus den folgenden Satzfragmenten Sätze mit Frageanhängseln.**

simple past: to listen to the CD – she

She listened to the CD, didn't she?

present perfect: not – to play golf – they

past progressive: to watch the movie – Vicky

simple past: to see a ghost – Zara

present perfect: not – to know the thief – Jack

simple past: to call the ambulance – the policeman

past progressive: to steal the bike – Luke

TESTEN

Klassenarbeit 2

45 Minuten

AUFGABE 6 **Finde das richtige Frageanhängsel *(question tag)* für die folgenden Aussagen.**

Tony played football two years ago,

Mr Smith hasn't phoned yet,

The children were singing Irish folk songs,

You didn't write those stories yesterday,

Elaine wasn't driving to Cardiff,

Robert and Lisa haven't been to Wales yet,

Dad is watching TV,

Peter, you didn't buy some milk,

AUFGABE 7 **Finde zu den unterstrichenen Satzteilen der folgenden Aussagesätze die richtigen Fragen. Achte dabei auf die Zeitform der Aussagesätze.**

Tim was reading comics yesterday afternoon.

Kim got up at six o'clock on Saturday.

The pupils in my class have just finished their project on animals.

My dog has already eaten all the dog biscuits.

I saw an exciting films last weekend.

The boys were swimming in the cold lake.

The Millers arrived too late.

AUFGABE 8 **Bilde aus den vorgegebenen Satzteilen Fragen in der richtigen Zeit. Schreibe in dein Übungsheft.**

simple past:
to be nervous – Tim
to buy the present – who
to buy the present – she – where
to sing – the pop star – many songs

present perfect:
to live in Sweden – they
to be – Tina – where

past progressive:
to read – she
to take pictures – she

AUFGABE 9 **Übersetze die folgenden Sätze.**

Wo verlor Mrs Green ihre Tasche?

Wann kam der Zug an *(to arrive)*?

Ich erzählte dir die Geschichte, oder nicht?

Las er das Buch? – Nein.

Spielten die Kinder im Garten?

Mr Smith ging gestern nicht zur Arbeit, nicht wahr?

Wer hat dieses Buch noch nicht gelesen?

Englisch lernen

7.1 Mit dem Wörterbuch umgehen

Zweisprachige Wörterbücher: Sie sind zweiteilig. In der einen Hälfte findest du die Übersetzung vom Englischen ins Deutsche, in der anderen die Übersetzung vom Deutschen ins Englische.	Englisch-Deutsch: abbreviation [abriːvɪ'eɪʃn]: Abkürzung Deutsch-Englisch: Abkürzung: a) (Weg) short cut; b) (Wort) abbreviation
Einsprachige Wörterbücher: Vorteil: Das englische Wort wird nur auf Englisch erläutert; du lernst so die Fremdsprache besser, da du ausschließlich mit englischen Wörtern arbeitest. Nachteil: Du kannst damit nicht vom Deutschen ins Englische übersetzen.	to roar: to make a loud and deep sound (a lion roars) pinkie: the smallest finger of a person's hand lollipop: a sweet on a small stick
Für die Arbeit mit dem Wörterbuch solltest du ■ das **Alphabet** perfekt beherrschen, ■ alle **Abkürzungen** verstehen, ■ die **phonetische Lautschrift** verstehen.	 Kommt *r* vor *v* oder nach *v*? adj. = adjective [ʃ] = „sch“
Anhand der Lautschrift erfährst du die Aussprache eines Wortes. Sie steht in eckigen Klammern hinter dem englischen Wort.	house [haʊs], brother ['brʌðə(r)], me [mɪ], example [ɪg'zɑːmpl]
Die meisten Wörterbücher haben einen **Anhang**. Hier findest du oft ■ eine Grundgrammatik, ■ eine Liste unregelmäßiger Verben, ■ Vorschläge für Briefformulierungen, ■ einen Überblick über die englischen und deutschen Maße und Gewichte, Zahlen, Datums- und Uhrzeitangaben.	 Nomen, Verben (*simple past*, *simple present* ...), Demonstrativpronomen ... irregular verbs: to go → went → gone “Dear Sally, ...” 1 mile = 1,61 km, 1 gallon = 4,546 l February 21st = 21. Februar

ÜBUNG 1 **Um rasch ein Wort im Wörterbuch zu finden, musst du fit im Alphabet sein.**

1. Trage den Buchstaben davor und danach ein. Beispiel: A B C

K	S	F	P	N	X
E	U	T	D	I	L

2. Wie heißt der drittnächste Buchstabe? Beispiel: V Y

D	T	J	C	I	O	N	E
S	Q	W	H	B	A	M	L

3. Wie heißt der vorletzte Buchstabe? Beispiel: F H

P	M	E	X	L	O	D	J
R	Z	N	S	W	T	F	C

WISSEN

Wörter im Wörterbuch finden
Ein Tipp zum schnelleren Auffinden eines gesuchten Wortes im Wörterbuch: Auf der linken Seite oben steht immer das erste Wort der Seite, auf der rechten Seite oben steht immer das letzte Wort der Seite. Diese Wörter heißen Leitwörter. So weißt du, welche Wörter auf dieser Seite dazwischen vorkommen.

ÜBUNG 2 **Im Folgenden stehen die beiden Leitwörter einer Seite im Wörterbuch. Unterstreiche die Wörter, die dazwischen passen.**

dumpling – ear: Dutch – dweller – eagle – edge – dualism – dusty – dump
headliner – heel: Hebrew – heavy – heftily – headship – hazard – hearty
meet – merrily: mental – meekly – medium – middle – meteor – menagerie
ideal – illusionist: illegally – illustrate – idol – idea – idiotic – identical – icy

ÜBUNG 3 **Suche die Übersetzung der rot markierten Wörter in einem Wörterbuch und schreibe sie neben die deutschen Wörter.**

rain:	Regentropfen		Regenbogen	
light:	Feuerzeug		Leuchtturm	
fish:	Fischstäbchen		Fischer	
back:	Rucksack		Hintergrund	

ÜBEN

ÜBUNG 4 **Hier werden dir unbekannte Wörter auf Englisch erklärt. Finde die richtige deutsche Übersetzung.**

gag – joke or funny story →

desert – land with very little water and a lot of sand (the Sahara Desert)

→

locker – cupboard where clothes can be put in (for example at a swimming-pool)

→

nickname – short form of a name (Michael → Mike) →

to kneel – to go down on your knees →

filly – a young female horse →

dormitory – large room with many beds →

chum – good old friend →

WISSEN

Die phonetische Lautschrift

Eine Besonderheit aller Wörterbücher ist die phonetische Lautschrift. Sie gibt an, wie ein Wort ausgesprochen wird. Es werden normale Buchstaben, aber auch besondere Zeichen verwendet. Merke dir die besonderen Zeichen am besten anhand eines einfachen Wortes!

Das englische Alphabet kennst du bereits aus Klasse 5. Du solltest es ständig wiederholen, damit du schnell buchstabieren kannst. Präge dir besonders ***a***, ***e*** und ***i*** ein.

a	[eɪ]	e	[iː]	i	[aɪ]	m	[em]	q	[kjuː]	u	[juː]	y	[waɪ]
b	[biː]	f	[ef]	j	[dʒeɪ]	n	[en]	r	[ɑː(r)]	v	[viː]	z	[zed]
c	[siː]	g	[dʒiː]	k	[keɪ]	o	[əʊ]	s	[es]	w	['dʌbljuː]		
d	[diː]	h	[eɪtʃ]	l	[el]	p	[piː]	t	[tiː]	x	[eks]		

[ŋ]	sing	[ɑː]	father	[aɪ]	fine, my
[r]	rose	[ʌ]	but, under	[aʊ]	now, house
[s]	class	[e]	pen	[eə]	there, pair
[z]	is	[ə]	a sister	[eɪ]	name, lay
[ʒ]	television	[ɜː]	girl	[ɪə]	here, nearly
[dʒ]	Germany, page	[æ]	fat	[ɔɪ]	boy
[ʃ]	ship	[ɪ]	bit	[əʊ]	old, hello
[tʃ]	chair, lunch	[iː]	easy, meet	[ʊə]	you're
[ð]	the	[ɒ]	got, on		
[θ]	thanks	[ɔː]	ball		
[v]	video, have	[ʊ]	book		
[w]	word, one	[uː]	too, two		

ÜBUNG 5 Mit deinem Wissen über die phonetische Lautschrift kannst du nun die folgenden Wörter erkennen.

['su:pəmɑ:kɪt] →
['neɪbə(r)] →
['bʌkɪt] →
['taɪmteɪbl] →
['vedʒɪtəbl] →
['hedeɪk] →
['prɒbəblɪ] →

WISSEN

Abkürzungen
Da jedes Wörterbuch Tausende von Wörtern besitzt, muss jeder Eintrag kurz gehalten werden. Deshalb werden viele Abkürzungen verwendet. Mach dich mit den Abkürzungen in deinem Wörterbuch vertraut! Ein Abkürzungsverzeichnis findest du meist vor dem Wörterverzeichnis.

ÜBUNG 6 Finde heraus, was die Abkürzungen bedeuten könnten.

complex: 1. **adj** kompliziert; 2. **n** Komplex
→ **adj** = , **n** =
men: **pl of** man
→ **pl of** =
receive: **vb** erhalten; empfangen
→ **vb** =
lift: *n* Aufzug (**Brit.**)
→ (**Brit.**) =
elevator: *n* Aufzug (**Amer.**)
→ (**Amer.**) =
¹elder: *n* Ältere
²elder: *n* Holunder
→ ¹/² =

7.2 Hörverstehen

Bevor du den Text hörst

Wenn du den Text einer Hörverstehensaufgabe anhörst, musst du nicht jedes Wort kennen bzw. verstehen, um die Aufgaben bearbeiten zu können. Manchmal kannst du die Bedeutung eines Wortes aus dem Zusammenhang erschließen.

Hier sind noch einige Tipps, die du beachten solltest:

Lies dir die Aufgabenstellung genau durch, um herauszufinden, ob du Lücken füllen musst, du die richtige Antwort ankreuzen sollst oder ob Fragen zu beantworten sind.

Höre dir das folgende Telefonat zweimal an und beantworte folgende Fragen.
Höre dir den folgenden Text an und kreuze die richtigen Antworten an.

Beim Durchlesen der Aufgabenstellung solltest du dich auch auf die **Art des Textes** einstellen, der in der Übung präsentiert wird. Es kann sich z. B. um einen Brief, einen Bericht oder ein Telefongespräch handeln.
Stelle dich auch auf die **Thematik** ein (ein Text über ein Land, eine Diskussion zu einer bestimmten Thematik).

Kim: Kim speaking.
Sarah: Hi Kim. Have you got a few minutes?
Kim: Yes, sure. What's the matter?
Sarah: Well, you know it's Robert's birthday next week and he's is going to have a party on Saturday.
Kim: I would never forget Robert's birthday.

Diese Vorüberlegungen sind hilfreich, weil du dir bereits **Vokabeln oder Formulierungen zurechtlegen** kannst, die du bei der Bearbeitung benötigst.

on the telephone – speaking
birthday – to have a party – invitation – present

Merke: Manchmal ist es auch hilfreich, wenn du dir eine Tabelle oder Liste anlegst.

Wähle für deine Notizen für dich verständliche Abkürzungen und Symbole, damit du nicht immer vollständige Sätze schreiben musst – das ist zeitlich meist nicht möglich.
Sicherlich hast du auch viele eigene Ideen, wie du deine Notizen kurzhalten kannst.

Großbuchstaben für Namen oder Eigennamen: S für Sam, M für Max, GB für Great Britain, Ger für Germany.
Einen Pfeil (→), wenn du zum Beispiel die Folge einer Handlung beschreiben möchtest: S played football → broke his arm.

Während du den Text hörst

Konzentriere dich auf den Text und auf das, was du hörst.

Gerate nicht in Panik, wenn du ein Wort oder ein Ausdruck nicht gleich verstehst. In einem Gespräch mit einem Briten oder Amerikaner wirst du auch nicht jedes einzelne Wort verstehen.
Versuche den Inhalt des Textes als Ganzes zu erfassen.

Mache dir auf einem Extrablatt **Notizen,** d. h., schreibe die Schlüsselwörter auf, die für die Beantwortung der Fragen wichtig sind. Manchmal helfen dir auch Symbole oder Abkürzungen, damit du keine Zeit verlierst.

Who? → Kim and Sarah
About what? → Robert's birthday
When? → on Saturday

Ergänze beim zweiten Hördurchgang Informationen, die dir fehlen.
Einige Hörverstehensaufgaben sind auch so angelegt, dass sie gleich beantwortet werden können. Dies gilt besonders für Ankreuzaufgaben.

Nachdem du den Text gehört hast

Beantworte in aller Ruhe die Fragen und **formuliere die Antworten in korrektem Englisch**. Achte dabei besonders auf die Satzstellung, die Zeitformen des Verbs und die Rechtschreibung.

Who is on the phone?
Sarah and Kim are on the phone.

What are they talking about?
They are talking about Robert's birthday.

Wähle bei der Beantwortung der Fragen immer die Zeitform, die auch in der Fragestellung verwendet wurde.

When is Robert going to have his party?
He is going to have his party on Saturday.

Wenn du dir noch immer unsicher bist, dann höre dir die CD noch einmal an – aber erst, wenn du alle Fragen zu einer Hörverstehensaufgabe bearbeitet hast.

ÜBUNG 7 **Höre dir Track 11 auf der CD an und schreibe die fehlenden Wörter in die Lücken.**

11

Hello, my name is Claire and I would like to talk about my school and ______ . I have been going to a ______ in Glasgow since last summer. My school is very big and there are about 900 ______ . I like it there and I have already become friendly with some of the girls. I'm in ______ 6 and I'm in the same ______ for all my ______ . You can learn two ______ at my school: ______ or ______ . My favourite subjects are ______ and P.E., which is ______ . The first ______ is at ten to nine. On Monday we have ______ and after that ______ from 9:50 a.m. to 10:50 a.m. Then there is a ______ and after that we have ______ and ______ . ______ is from 1:10 p.m. to 2:10 p.m. and you can buy something to eat in the ______ or you can bring a ______ . We have ______ lessons from 2:10 p.m. to 3:20 p.m. After the afternoon lessons have finished I sometimes stay for my ______ – I play ______ every Wednesday.

ÜBUNG 8 **Höre dir Track 12 auf der CD an – auch zwei- oder dreimal. Kreuze an, ob die Sätze richtig oder falsch sind. Korrigiere die, die nicht richtig sind, in deinem Übungsheft.**

12

	right	wrong
1. Max is going to visit Sam during his Easter holidays.	☐	☐
2. Sam has got a brother called George and a sister called Janet.	☐	☐
3. George is older than Sam.	☐	☐
4. Sam is good at German.	☐	☐
5. Sam revises his German vocabulary regularly.	☐	☐
6. Sam hopes that the weather will be fine around Easter.	☐	☐
7. Max should bring along his roller skates.	☐	☐
8. Max has been playing tennis for about three years.	☐	☐

DUDEN

Einfach klasse in

Englisch

Lösungsheft

6.

Klasse

1 Adjektive und Adverbien

ÜBUNG 1 **S. 6**

nice – terrible – happy – short –
expensive – soft – hard – cheap – tall – big – rich

ÜBUNG 2 **S. 6**

a tall woman – a small car – an exciting computer game – a high mountain – a funny joke – a red tomato – a long train – a bad dream

ÜBUNG 3 **S. 6**

Mount Everest is higher than the Zugspitze. The Zugspitze is not as high as Mount Everest.
A mouse is smaller than an elephant. An elephant is not as small as a mouse.
My granddad is older than my mum. My mum is not as old as my granddad.
Maths is more difficult than biology. Biology is not as difficult as maths.
A computer is more expensive than a mobile phone. A mobile phone is not as expensive as a computer.

ÜBUNG 4 **S. 7**

My sister is more beautiful. She's the most beautiful girl in the world.
I'm cleverer. I'm the cleverest boy / girl in class.
My bike is faster. It's the fastest bike in town.
I'm happier. I'm the happiest person on earth.
hat film is better. It's the best film ever.
y dog is lazier. It is the laziest dog in the orld.
ly brother is taller. He is the tallest person in ur family.

ÜBUNG 5 **S. 8**

attributiver Gebrauch:
The **young** lady likes chocolate.
She loves her **new** ring.
They're wearing **cool** sunglasses.
prädikativer Gebrauch:
Tim looks **sad**.
The table is **big**.
My friends feel **happy**.

ÜBUNG 6 **S. 8**

Tina is tall, but Jenny is taller. Jenny is as tall as Ben.
Be careful. You must be more careful than yesterday.
In April the weather is bad, but in November it's worse. In January it's worst.
I am as clever as ... .

ÜBUNG 7 **S. 10**

My grandmother speaks **quietly**.
The people laughed **loudly**.
You can guess the answer **easily**.
She walked **slowly** out of the room.
Manchester United played **badly** and lost the match.

ÜBUNG 8 **S. 10**

loud → loudly
quiet → quietly
good → well
happy → happily
careful → carefully
nervous → nervously
nice → nicely
lucky → luckily

ÜBUNG 9 **S. 10**

Mark drinks quickly.
Christy dances well.
Simon shouts angrily.
They play soccer badly.
Peggy smiles happily.
I speak English well.

ÜBUNG 10 **S. 11**

A	L	N	P	W	E	X	T	R	E	M	E	L	Y	V	I	Q	A	R
E	E	S	X	Z	J	P	L	K	O	T	G	C	S	D	Y	S	J	Z
B	A	G	J	Y	I	V	A	T	U	R	D	H	Z	R	T	A	B	X
F	S	K	W	M	O	X	Q	M	Y	H	S	F	C	D	O	C	X	W
H	I	L	E	N	G	R	H	A	P	P	I	L	Y	U	D	Z	L	B
M	L	R	L	F	B	F	E	E	G	E	T	C	D	K	A	M	B	L
T	Y	O	L	F	W	U	C	I	R	Q	B	A	D	L	Y	J	M	I
N	Q	E	H	P	V	P	J	N	S	E	P	B	D	U	V	N	O	Z
M	U	I	O	F	T	E	N	H	K	Q	H	F	X	O	W	C	G	A
L	A	D	K	K	T	J	I	O	C	A	R	E	F	U	L	L	Y	Y

ÜBUNG 11 **S. 11**

to watch	carefully	more carefully	most carefully
to cycle	well	better	best
to speak	clearly	more clearly	most clearly
to write	badly	worse	worst
to speak	slowly	more slowly	most slowly
to play volleyball	well	better	best
to talk	loudly	more loudly	most loudly

ÜBUNG 12 **S. 11**

Betty plays tennis perfectly.
Christy dances well.
John speaks nervously.
It rains heavily in October.
They read carefully.
My father cooks fantastically.

ÜBUNG 13 **S. 12**

Dear Peter,
How are you? I hope you are doing as **well** as I am. Let me tell you about a great day. Yesterday, I went to a birthday party. At the beginning I stood **sadly** alone because I didn't know anybody. But then some boys and girls came over and talked to me. We played badminton in the garden.
I played **well** but the others played much **better**. I was on a good team, so we won the match **easily**.
When it got dark, we made a bonfire **quickly**. One of the boys played the guitar. We sang "Happy Birthday" **loudly** and started dancing **wildly**. It was so much fun. But the best part of the evening was the fireworks at the end. Everyone watched **excitedly**.
Write back soon!
Yours, Mark

ÜBUNG 14 **S. 12**

I often go to the cinema.
I speak English well.
Martin usually gets up at 7 o'clock.
I play basketball badly.

ÜBUNG 15 **S. 14**

A VW Beetle is a **slow** car.
A VW Beetle driver drives **slowly**.
It's a **sad** story.
He tells the story **sadly**.
Tim is very **nervous**.
He talks **nervously**.
Lisa is a **quiet** girl.
She talks **quietly**.

ÜBUNG 16 **S. 14**

Lösungsvorschlag (es sind auch andere Adjektive und Adverbien denkbar):
This is a nice / fast / modern car. It drives fast / slowly.
He's a happy/nice/bad boy. He works carefully / well / badly.
The basketball match is funny / exciting / boring. The players play badly / well.

ÜBUNG 17 **S. 14**

A cheetah is a **fast (Adj.)** animal.
A panther runs **fast (Adv.)**, too.
Richard is a **hard (Adj.)** worker. Susan works **hard (Adv.)**, too. But Tim **hardly (Adv.)** works at all.
Anne is a **pretty (Adj.)** girl. She talks **pretty (Adv.)** cool. And she laughs **prettily (Adv.)**.
Marc is a **good (Adj.)** volleyball player. And Kim plays **well (Adv.)**, too.
How are you feeling today? – I'm **well (Adj.)** again, thank you.

ÜBUNG 18 **S. 15**

The soup smells **good**.
David has got a cold. He can't smell **well**.
The fish tastes **bad**.
Marc tastes the meal **carefully**.
George looks at his brother **angrily**.
Linda isn't happy at all. She looks very **angry**.

ÜBUNG 19 **S. 15**

My brother is taller than my sister.
The old lady looks pretty unhappy.
It was the worst day of my life: Someone stole my new bike and I had a terrible toothache.
Computer games are not as interesting as going on a dangerous trip.
It was night. Teresa hardly saw anything.

ÜBUNG 20 **S. 15**

I get up early every morning.
My father drives faster than my mother.
Rita looks sad. She feels bad.
You speak English well.

Klassenarbeiten

AUFGABE 1 **S. 16**

(siehe unten)

AUFGABE 2 **S. 16**

	Adjektiv	Adverb
vorsichtig	careful	carefully
furchtbar	terrible	terribly
früh	early	early
einfach	simple	simply
fantastisch	fantastic	fantastically
schnell	fast	fast

AUFGABE 3 **S. 16**

Great (Adj.) fun and **better (Adj.)** marks
Do you want to improve your English **quickly (Adv.)** and make **new (Adj.)** friends around the world? If yes, then join our **interesting (Adj.)** exchange programme and spend your holiday in **beautiful (Adj.)** Great Britain!
You live **comfortably (Adv.)** with **nice (Adj.)** families. In the morning you'll study English in groups with **friendly (Adj.)** teachers. In the afternoons we'll take you on **exciting (Adj.)** trips. You'll visit **important (Adj.)** sights, take part in **different (Adj.)** sports activities, and meet **new (Adj.)** friends **quickly (Adv.)**. Isn't this the **perfect (Adj.)** way to learn English? If you are interested, please contact "FunTours".

AUFGABE 4 **S. 17**

Dear Jennifer Lopez,
My name is Gina and I am a **big** fan of yours. I think you are very **pretty** and that you dance **beautifully**. I would like to dance as **well** as you. Last year I started dancing lessons. The instructor is very **strict** but I am getting **better quickly**.
My **secret** wish is to dance **professionally** in one of your shows. How did you start your **wonderful** career? Please give me some **helpful** advice.
Your fan Gina

AUFGABE 5 **S. 17**

Richard opens his bag slowly.
My dad is a careful driver.
It is a fast train. It travels very fast.
Betty is pretty clever.
Harry works very hard. He hardly sleeps.
Jim dances very well. He is a good dancer.

AUFGABE 1

	Positiv	Komparativ	Superlativ
groß	big	bigger	biggest
glücklich	happy	happier	happiest
gefährlich	dangerous	more dangerous	most dangerous
gut	good	better	best
schlecht	bad	worse	worst

AUFGABE 6 **S. 18**

good	better	best
carefully	more carefully	most carefully
bad / badly	worse	worst
terribly	more terribly	most terribly
easy	easier	easiest
great	greater	greatest
slowly	more slowly	most slowly
narrow	narrower	narrowest
expensive	more expensive	most expensive

AUFGABE 7 **S. 18**

Jenny feels **better than** yesterday but not **well** enough to go to school.
Sarah looked around **nervously** and started to speak **quietly**.
Jenny's mother opened the letter **carefully**. It was a **long** letter with **beautiful** handwriting.
Mum drives **faster than** dad. She is not **as careful as** he is.
The police did a **good** job. They did their job very **well**.

AUFGABE 8 **S. 19**

Mr Smith is an old teacher.
Los Angeles is a famous city.
Brad Pitt is a good-looking actor.
Ants are small animals.

AUFGABE 9 **S. 19**

Angelina Jolie is **prettier** than our teacher.
My mum is **younger** than my friend's mum.
Mr Bond is **more handsome** than our neighbour.
The A 380 Airbus is **the biggest** airplane in the world.
My Dad is **stronger** than me.
Our school is **the ugliest** building in town.
A cat is **more intelligent** than a fish.

AUFGABE 10 **S. 19**

Art und Weise: slowly, carefully, happily, simply, basically, badly
Zeit: today, lately, already, tomorrow
Ort: there, here, everywhere

AUFGABE 11 **S. 20**

It is not **easy** to write a book.
Please remember to ride your bike **carefully**.
You often drive too **quickly**.
My mum is very **unhappy** because I don't write my homework **tidily**.
Dennis feels **nervous** because he has a dentist's appointment in the afternoon.
The bus arrived **late** again and so I missed the beginning of the show.
Pupils often think that they work **harder** than their teachers.

AUFGABE 12 **S. 20**

Peter went outside yesterday.
Every weekday, Mr Smith arrives at the office at 8:30 a.m.
You should definitely stop smoking!
He ate and drank a lot last week.

AUFGABE 13 **S. 20**

My dad speaks English very badly.
Lilly plays the violoncello well.
They sang the "Happy-Birthday"-song loudly.
She excitedly waited for her friend.
The meal smells good.
Mother looks quite angry.

2 Modale Hilfsverben

ÜBUNG 1 **S. 22**

I can ride a horse. I cannot / can't ride an elephant.
I can speak English. I cannot / can't speak Chinese.
I can repair a bike. I cannot / can't repair a car.
I can go to Italy. I cannot / can't got to the moon.
I can drink lemonade. I cannot / can't drink beer.

ÜBUNG 2 **S. 22**
Could / can you give me the book, please?
Thomas and Tina **can** do a lot of tricks.
When I was young I **could** walk on my hands. I **cannot / can't** do it now.
You **can** take my old bike. But you **cannot / can't** use my new bike.
King Edward lived from 1239–1307. He **could** speak different languages. But he **could not / couldn't** use a computer. They had no computers around 1300.

ÜBUNG 3 **S. 22**
Last year we **could / were able to** go to India.
At the moment Marc **can't / cannot / isn't able to** play the guitar. But he has got a teacher now. Next year he **will be able to** play the guitar.
Toby **couldn't / could not / wasn't able to** ride a bike when he was three. But now he's twelve, so he **is able to / can** ride a bike.
Can you **/ Are** you **able to** climb Mount Everest?

ÜBUNG 4 **S. 24**
I am allowed to go swimming.
I am not allowed to run fast.
I am allowed to sing a love song.
I am not allowed to play a computer game.
I am not allowed to watch the show.
I am allowed to do the washing-up.
I am allowed to watch a film on TV.
I am not allowed to go to the party.

ÜBUNG 5 **S. 24**
You **are not allowed to** turn left, but you **are allowed to** turn right.
May I help you with your work?
She **was not allowed to** borrow the skateboard last week.
Were you allowed to watch TV last week?
Dogs **are not allowed** in the cinema.
You **mustn't** bring your dog.
Visitors **may not** use their mobile phones during the show.

ÜBUNG 6 **S. 24**
Jane was allowed to visit us.
Tom will not be allowed to stay.
Is he allowed to come with us?

ÜBUNG 7 **S. 26**
Mum: "Pit, after school you **must clean** your bike! Then you **must do your homework**. You **must show** it to your father in the evening. At 5 o'clock you **must do the shopping**. And at 9 o'clock you **must go to bed**. You **must get up** early tomorrow!"

ÜBUNG 8 **S. 26**
Pit: "Then I had to do my homework.
I had to show it to my father in the evening.
At 5 o'clock I had to do the shopping. And at 9 o'clock I had to go to bed. I had to get up early this morning."

ÜBUNG 9 **S. 26**
My teacher is very strict. I **have to** do my homework.
I have been running for one hour. I **must** drink something.
Mother to Jill: "Don't be late! You **must** be home at 10 o'clock!" – Jill to her friends: "I **have to** be home at 10. My mother told me so."

ÜBUNG 10 **S. 27**
Can we help you, sir? – No, you cannot / can't help me.
Is he allowed to take your bike? – No, he is not allowed to take this bike.
May I have a bottle of coke, please? – No, you may not have a bottle of coke.
Will she be allowed to call me tomorrow? – No, she will not / won't be allowed to call you tomorrow.
Were you able to repair the fridge? – No, we were not/weren't able to repair the fridge.
Can you see the moon? – No, I cannot / can't see the moon.

ÜBUNG 11 **S. 28**
Instructor: "Good morning everyone. How do you feel after your first day of snowboarding?"
Betty: "I feel good today but I **had to** go to bed early yesterday. I was so tired."
Instructor: "That's alright. On your first day you **had to** learn all the basics. Today we will practise a lot. Remember, tomorrow **you will have to** pass a test. So we **have to** start right away."
John: "Can we put on our snowboards right now? Or **do we have to** have a warming-up first?"
Instructor: "Of course you always **have (got) to** do a warming-up first. Today you **have (got) to** get up the hill with the lift. To use the lift – what **do you have to** do?"
Steven: "We **have to** stand on the snowboard with one foot only."
Instructor: "You're right. Good luck – I will see you on the top of the hill."

ÜBUNG 12 **S. 29**
you don't have to go
you needn't help
you mustn't drink
you needn't pay
you don't have to go
I mustn't stay up

ÜBUNG 13 **S. 29**
"I must go now." / "I have to go now."
"You needn't help me."
"Can I open the window?" / "May I open the window?"
"I couldn't do my homework yesterday." /
"I wasn't able to do my homework yesterday."
"Can I ask a question?" / "May I ask a question?"
"You must be quiet." / "You have to be quiet."

Klassenarbeiten

AUFGABE 1 **S. 30**
May I have a glass of water, please? → höfliche Bitte
The bus mustn't stop here. → striktes Verbot
You can do your homework later. → Möglichkeit
You must be careful. → Aufforderung
Willy was able to dance. → Fähigkeit
Are we allowed to listen? → Erlaubnis

AUFGABE 2 **S. 30**
You mustn't sit here. / You are not allowed to sit here.
You must wear a helmet. / You have to wear a helmet.
May I help you?
You don't have to wait for me.
You needn't do the washing-up.
You are allowed to watch the film.
Can you speak Chinese?

AUFGABE 3 **S. 31**
1. Tom was able to ride a motor bike.
Tom will be able to ride a motor bike.
2. She had to write a story.
She will have to write a story.
3. I was allowed to go camping with my friends.
I will be allowed to go camping with my friends.
4. Richard and Diana did not / didn't have to come.
Richard and Diana will not / won't have to come.

AUFGABE 4 **S. 31**
I wasn't allowed to watch TV
did you have to wait
we weren't able to open
will you be able to sing

AUFGABE 5 **S. 31**
Did you have to work yesterday?
Will you be able to come tomorrow?
Laila needn't go to bed.
May / Can I ask you a question?
Was Dean allowed to listen?
Vera mustn't / isn't allowed to come.
Does she have to drink tea?

AUFGABE 6 **S. 32**
I can / I am able to; they could / were able to; you will be allowed to; we were allowed to; I did not have to; you will have to

AUFGABE 7 **S. 32**
Peter can swim and do karate, but he can't play the violin or ride a unicycle.
Jamie can play the violin, ride a unicycle and swim, but he can't do karate.
Helena can ride a unicycle and swim, but she can't play the violin or do karate.
Vicky can do karate, but she can't play the violin, ride a unicycle or swim.
Robin can't play the violin, ride a unicycle or do karate, but he can swim.

AUFGABE 8 **S. 33**
Do you want to see a movie tonight? I'd really like, but I can't. I **have to** study for my math exam.
Did you go to school yesterday? No, I didn't. I was ill and **had to** stay in bed. I **was not able to** get up and watch TV.
I went shopping yesterday. I really **had to** buy a new pair of jeans because I tore my favourite jeans in a bike accident.
My leg is broken. I **am not able to** do any sports for four weeks.
Mother to her daughter: You **will be allowed to** go to that party next weekend if you help me tidy up the kitchen.
May I smoke? No, you **mustn't** smoke inside here. This is a non-smoking building.
I can't go out tonight. I **have to** finish my essay.

AUFGABE 9 **S. 33**
You **must** have a passport when you travel to the USA.
You **needn't** exchange Euro money when you travel to Slovakia.
You **mustn't** be late for school.
You mustn't smoke inside this building.

AUFGABE 10 **S. 33**
I can speak French. Can I help you?
We could go to the cinema.
Jane isn't allowed to go to Peter's party.
I must tidy my room today.
I had to tidy my room yesterday.
I am really hungry. I need to eat something right now.
In court, you have to tell truth.

3 Vergangenheit

ÜBUNG 1 **S. 35**
Two thousand years ago, people **lived** differently. They **owned** no cars and **used** no mobile phones. They **talked** about different things and **liked** different clothes.

ÜBUNG 2 **S. 35**
washed, played, watched, opened, entered, phoned, liked, stayed

ÜBUNG 3 **S. 35**
to worry → worried [d], to work → worked [t], to stop → stopped [t], to wait → waited [ɪd], to tidy → tidied [d], to arrive → arrived [d], to live → lived [d], to like → liked [d]

ÜBUNG 4 **S. 36**

Dear Bill,
Last week I **travelled** from Germany to London with my class. We saw a lot of buildings and places, and on our last day we **visited** Madame Tussaud's, the wax figure museum. We **looked** at all the wax figures of famous people, for example the Queen, Madonna, and Michael Jackson. We had our cameras with us and had a lot of fun. When we **entered** another room, somebody **shouted**: "Elvis lives!" We **turned** around and could see the Elvis figure. We were very frightened because suddenly Elvis **started** to move and play the guitar. When the shock was over, we **started** to laugh: It was just a joke – we **noticed** that Elvis was just an actor.
Hope to hear from you soon!
Yours, Peter

ÜBUNG 5 **S. 36**

simple past	**Grundform mit *to***
travelled	to travel
visited	to visit
looked	to look
entered	to enter
shouted	to shout
turned	to turn
started	to start
noticed	to notice

ÜBUNG 6 **S. 36**

Susan watered the flowers.
Toby tidied his room.
Susan and Toby cleaned the kitchen.
Toby repaired his bike.
Susan played with the dogs.
Susan worked with her father.
They watched TV in the evening.

ÜBUNG 7 **S. 39**

U	P	A	T	S	U	O	S	N	M	B	Y	C	A	Z
L	V	W	B	U	I	L	T	I	H	J	G	B	Y	B
V	Q	K	R	S	X	N	O	L	J	D	D	O	K	E
X	D	Y	R	B	T	W	O	X	C	R	B	U	F	A
F	R	E	Q	F	D	E	D	J	H	E	Z	G	Z	L
H	A	Z	C	M	W	D	L	K	H	W	V	H	P	M
G	N	A	P	R	O	D	E	C	G	B	O	T	S	Y
O	K	I	Q	W	J	F	K	V	I	X	R	N	U	U
R	N	D	G	N	C	O	U	L	D	P	Q	O	F	A
E	V	S	P	M	L	C	O	X	R	Q	G	B	D	T
Y	T	K	N	E	W	N	D	O	Y	T	A	C	I	Z
U	U	M	M	K	O	E	W	S	R	A	V	B	D	E
Z	A	N	L	X	T	G	W	R	O	T	E	T	C	S
V	F	O	U	N	D	H	G	I	J	F	G	Z	D	A
J	K	K	F	L	I	J	S	M	F	E	Q	D	F	R

***simple past*-Form**	**Grundform**
built	to build
drank	to drink
knew	to know
found	to find
wrote	to write
could	can
stood	to stand
drew	to draw
bought	to buy
gave	to give
did	to do
rode	to ride

ÜBUNG 8 **S. 39**

Did they go to the shop? → Yes, they went to the shop. / No, they didn't go to the shop.
Did Tina lose her purse? → Yes, she lost her purse. / No, she didn't lose her purse.
Did they clean the room? → Yes, they cleaned the room. / No, they didn't clean the room.
Did Sandra buy a book? → Yes, she bought a book. / No, she didn't buy a book.
Did you drink a milk shake? → Yes, I drank a milk shake. / No, I didn't drink a milk shake.

ÜBUNG 9 **S. 40**
1. Tom and Tina were happy.
2. My family had a big dog.
3. It was very funny.
4. Yesterday we were at home.
5. He had a cold.
6. Last Monday I was ill.
7. Last summer Frank worked at the zoo.

ÜBUNG 10 **S. 40**
On Monday, I **visited** my friend Susan. She **was** ill. I **helped** her with her homework, but she **knew** all the answers herself. Her mother **gave** us some drinks and some sandwiches. In the evening, I **played** Monopoly with my brother. I **went** to bed early, but I **couldn't** sleep.
On Tuesday, I **went** to see the dentist because I **had** some problems with my teeth. After that my mother **bought** me a new shirt.
On Wednesday, I **wrote** an English test. In the afternoon I **did** my homework. Then I **ate** some chocolate and **drank** some tea. In the evening, I **watched** a film about Africa.
On Thursday, I **woke** up at 7:30 a.m. I **was** late, so I **ran** to school. I really **had to** hurry!
On Friday, I **did not have to** go to school because our teacher **was** ill. She **had** a bad cold, just like Susan on Monday. So I **got** up at 10 a.m.

ÜBUNG 11 **S. 42**
Last Sunday we **had** *(simple past)* dinner. After dinner we **played** *(simple past)* a game and **talked** *(simple past)* about the day. We **went** *(simple past)* to bed early.
While we **were listening** *(past progressive)* to the concert they **stole** *(simple past)* my bike.
Ellen **was walking** *(past progressive)* home when she **met** *(simple past)* Dennis.
His friends **were waiting** *(past progressive)* in the kitchen while Tom **was cleaning** *(past progressive)* his room.

ÜBUNG 12 **S. 42**
Sandra was watching TV.
Tina was eating a banana.
Rick was writing an e-mail.
They were doing their homework.
Tim was listening to music.
Sarah and Jane were skating.

ÜBUNG 13 **S. 43**
I **was eating** a sandwich when the phone **rang**.
When Tina **entered** the restaurant, her family **was waiting** there.
While they **were sitting** in the waiting room, the door **opened** and an old lady **came** in.
Mum **came** home while I **was playing** with our dog.
Ryan **was doing** his homework when Mr Miller **called**.

ÜBUNG 14 **S. 43**
While Kitty was having a shower, Marc came home.
I was playing volleyball when Harry told me the news.
George and Emily were laughing when the taxi arrived.
The boys were playing football while the girls were skating in the park.
Mr Stevenson was talking to his friend when he saw the accident.

ÜBUNG 15 **S. 43**
Mr Miller was crossing the street when the accident happened.
While she was playing in the garden, it began to rain.
Tom and Philipp were doing their homework while Mrs Jones was cooking.
I was writing a letter to grandma when the postman rang at the door.

ÜBUNG 17

1 HE HAS STOPPED
2 WE HAVE WATCHED
3 YOU HAVE TRIED
4 HE HAS LAUGHED
5 HE HAS CYCLED
6 SHE HAS ALLOWED
7 SHE HAS LOOKED
8 WE HAVE CLOSED
9 HE HAS PULLED
10 I HAVE LIVED
11 SHE HAS WASHED
12 THEY HAVE WORRIED
13 WE HAVE LOVED
14 HE HAS DANCED

ÜBUNG 16 **S. 46**
eaten – drink – **thought** – **shown** – sang – spoke – **driven** – eat – **gone** – **done** – break – have – knew – were – write – **written** – fall – keep – know – **drunk** – **slept** – show – ring – **rung** – begin – **begun** – **been** – was – **stolen** – became – laugh – rang – **taken** – **met**

ÜBUNG 17 **S. 46**
(siehe oben)
Lösungssatz: Eve has played with the dogs.

ÜBUNG 18 **S. 47**
Ida's bike is shining. She **has** just **cleaned** it.
Have you **done** your homework? – Yes, I **have** already **finished** it.
Jim **has had to** take his medicine.
Look here, my hands are clean. I **have** just **washed** them.
We have English at school. I **have learned / learnt** it for two years.
Marc **has lived** in Berlin for three years now.
We **haven't been** to France yet.
Jane and Tim **have read** the magazines. They don't need them anymore.

ÜBUNG 19 **S. 47**

						1				4
				3		S				F
				A		I				O
				L	2	N	E	V	E	R
				R		C				
			5	E	V	E	R			
				A						
				D						
6 N	O	T		Y	E	T				

ÜBUNG 20 **S. 47**
Gina has just written a letter.
I have never listened to Indian music.
Harry and Kim have worked in a restaurant for nine months.
We have already been able to book our trip to Paris. / We have been able to book our trip to Paris already.
He hasn't been allowed to go to London yet.

ÜBUNG 21 **S. 48**
They have just finished their work.
Rosa has lived in Rome for two years.
She has just cleaned the windows.
I have already listened to the CD.

ÜBUNG 22 S. 48

since (Zeitpunkt)	*for* (Zeitraum)
since yesterday	for two years
since 1984	for one hour
since last October	for ten months
since 9 o'clock	for the last two weeks
since Friday	for a long time
since January 1st	for six days
since Chistmas	for one minute

ÜBUNG 23 S. 49

She has written a birthday card.
He has made his bed.
I have done my homework.
The dogs have eaten the cake.
Michael has listened to the new CD.
They have bought a present.
She has read the newspaper.

ÜBUNG 24 S. 49

They have walked all the way home.
He has eaten chocolate cake.
Ruth has had an accident.
I have forgotten his birthday.

ÜBUNG 25 S. 50

I have eaten Chinese food since I was ten years old.
Julia and Ron have known each other since 2007.
The girls have talked on the phone for three hours.

ÜBUNG 26 S. 50

The Greens and the Sanders are planing to go to the adventure park. It's 8 o'clock in the morning.
Gina Green: "Mum, dad, wake up! We **have overslept**. I **haven't heard** the alarm clock. Lisa **has** just **called**. The Sanders **have** already **left**."
(...)
Dad: "I **have prepared** the picnic. **Have** you **taken** a shower, Gina?"
Gina: "Yes, I **have** just **finished** in the bathroom. It's your turn now. **Have** you **packed** some biscuits and a bottle of water?"
Dad: "Yes, I **have put** everything in the bag. But I **haven't found** our swimsuits."
Mum: "I **have** just **seen** them on the table over there.
Gina: "Listen, the phone is ringing! Lisa **has called** again. The Sanders **have turned** back home because they **have forgotten** their money."

ÜBUNG 27 S. 50

I have already read the book.
My mum has just called.
Kate has played golf for four years.
Richard has already bought flowers.

ÜBUNG 28 S.53

simple past	*past progressive*	*present perfect*
threw	was eating	have drawn
went	were going	has gone
listened	were doing	has bought
visited	was cleaning	have seen
lost	was wearing	has slept
did	were having	have told

ÜBUNG 29 S. 53

past progressive: Gina **was watching** TV and Andrew **was sitting** next to her.
While they **were walking** home, a bus passed them.
simple past: At 8 o'clock I **ate** some bread, **drank** a cup of tea and **took** the bus.
present perfect: Uncle John **has written** six postcards since he left.
I **have** just **turned** off the radio.

ÜBUNG 30 S. 54

to look – **looked** – have looked – **to write** – wrote – **have written** – to see – **saw** – **have seen** – **to run** – **ran** – have run – to talk – **talked** – **have talked** – **to throw** – threw – **have thrown** – **to give** – gave – **have given** – **to ask** – **asked** – have asked – to meet – **met** – **have met** – **to pull** – pulled – **have pulled** –

ÜBUNG 31 S. 54

Last Christmas we **had** turkey for dinner.
Sarah **wrote** the e-mail two weeks ago.
Grandma **has** just **arrived**.
Max and Tina **went** to England last year.
Dana **has been** to England **for** three months.
Mum **wore** her new dress last Sunday.
Victor **has** never **worn** his new jeans so far.
The Millers **have painted** their house in March. It is pink and yellow now.

ÜBUNG 32 S. 55

1. Yesterday Gina **ate** pizza for dinner.
Rachel **has eaten** pizza for the last three days.
I **was eating** pizza when Eddy **came** along.
2. While Emma **was walking** to school, she **met** Sam.
I **walked** home yesterday.
She **has** just **walked** through the door.
3. He **has** just **written** the letter.
I **was writing** a postcard when the phone **rang**.
They **wrote** an e-mail two weeks ago.

ÜBUNG 33 S. 55

While we were sitting in the park, a dog jumped at us.
They were working in the garden when a mouse ran through the bushes.
While Joan was selling clothes in a shop, someone stole a shirt.
I was riding my bike in the forest when a rabbit crossed my path.
While they were taking pictures, the battery died.
Liz was watching a film when someone screamed.
While Sally was reading the newspapers, she suddenly discovered her dad's name.

Klassenarbeiten

AUFGABE 1 S. 56

Father has **just** arrived here. → *present perfect*
Verena bought a new board **two weeks ago.** → *simple past*
I have learned English **for two years**. → *present perfect*
While the baby was playing, its mother ... → *past progressive*
Have you **ever** seen a Shakespeare play? → *present perfect*
We walked all the way to the city centre **on Monday**. → *simple past*
Tony has played the piano **for one hour**. → *present perfect*

AUFGABE 2 S. 56

Grundform	*simple past*	*past participle*
to run	ran	run
to buy	bought	bought
to be	was/were	been
to think	thought	thought
to write	wrote	written
to know	knew	known
to leave	left	left
to speak	spoke	spoken
to tell	told	told
to meet	met	met
to stand	stood	stood
to win	won	won
to get	got	got
to give	gave	given
to do	did	done

AUFGABE 3 **S. 57**

While Lena **was sleeping**, the dog suddenly **barked**.
Rosa **was sitting** at the lake when someone **screamed**.
While Mrs Turner **was waiting** for the bus and Tina **was talking** to her best friend, an accident **happened**.
They **were eating** ice cream when the thief **took** the bag.
I **was reading** a book and my brother **was studying**.
The boys **were playing** cards when the bell rang.

AUFGABE 4 **S. 57**

Signalwörter für *simple past*	Signalwörter für *present perfect*
yesterday	so far
last week	since last July
one week ago	for two days
in 1983	never
last year	just
last summer	already

AUFGABE 5 **S. 58**

Das *past progressive* wird verwendet, um den **Ablauf** einer Handlung zu betonen. Signalwörter sind: **while, when**
Das *simple past* wird verwendet, wenn eine Handlung in der **Vergangenheit** abgeschlossen ist. Signalwörter sind: **yesterday, last year, one week ago**
Das *present perfect* wird verwendet, wenn eine Handlung in der **Vergangenheit** begonnen hat und in der **Gegenwart** noch von Bedeutung ist. Signalwörter sind: **since, for, just, already, yet**

AUFGABE 6 **S. 58**

Susan and Lisa **were riding** their bikes when the rain **started**.
Benny **has learned** three languages **since** 2001.
My friends **have** just **arrived** at the restaurant.
Leonardo da Vinci **painted** the Mona Lisa in 1503.
The girls **were talking** to each other while the boys **were playing** with the dogs.
I **bought** the tomatoes three days ago.
The family **has lived** in America **for** ten years now.
Mrs George **has** already **read** three books by John Steinbeck.

AUFGABE 7 **S. 59**

past progressive; present progressive; simple past; present perfect

AUFGABE 8 **S. 59**

he drank; they were seeing; we had; she is reading; I watched; you were leaving

AUFGABE 9 **S. 59**

Mary has finished her homework.
Mr Miller has washed his car.
Lilly has written a letter.
The guests have eaten a delicious meal.
Grandma has baked a cake.

AUFGABE 10 **S. 60**

Have you ever swum in the Atlantic Ocean? Yes, I have. I swum in the Atlantic Ocean last year.
Have you ever played beach volleyball? No, I haven't.
Have you ever been skiing? Yes, I have. I went skiing last Christmas.
Have you ever ridden a mountainbike? Yes, I have. I rode a mountainbike last summer in Switzerland.
Have you ever drunk champagne? Yes, I have. I drank champagne on my 14th birthday.
Have you ever lost a pair of shoes? Yes, I have. I lost a pair of shoes last summer.

AUFGABE 11 **S. 60**

Mother came in to Mia's room while she **was crying.**
What are you doing at the moment? – I **am washing** the dishes.
While Laura **was waiting** for her school bus, she **saw** an accident happen.
When Hannah **was** a little girl, her family **had lived** in New Zealand for three years.
The sun **rises** every morning.
Lilly **had finished** her homework before her father came home.
Mother **has visited** grandmother in hospital twice since last Friday.
Two years ago, while John **was travelling** through Australia, an earthquake happened.

AUFGABE 12 **S. 60**

My sister has lived in Ireland for two years.
Did Laura go to Peter's party yesterday?
Mary has played the piano for five years.
Who told you that story?
Yesterday I went to the cinema and ate ice-cream.

AUFGABE 13 **S. 61**

keep; forgotten; put; rode; ridden; bought; ate; done

AUFGABE 14 **S. 61**

A year ago my friends and I **took** the train to Scotland. We **went** with other children from our youth club. Tessa and I **organised** the holiday. Our club leader **helped**, of course. We **stayed** in tents. We **cooked** our own meals. We **walked** to a lot of interesting places there. We **had** a lot of fun. I really **liked** last year's holidays!

AUFGABE 15 **S. 61**

When Peter's mother **came** into Peter's room she **saw** that he and his friends **were playing** a computer game. She **told** them to stop. Peter, however, **told** his mother that they **were playing** a harmless game and **asked** his mother to leave his room. Peter's mother **got** very angry. She **left** the room, but **gave** her son a fierce glance.

AUFGABE 16 **S. 62**

When did Mary read a book?
Where did Lisa travel to last summer?
Whose book did Sarah take?
Who stole your bike?
Why did you stay home last Friday night?'
Whom do you want to speak to?
What did Megan see?

AUFGABE 17 **S. 62**

Last Saturday,
the dog was chasing the cat,
Mr Miller was washing the dishes,
the children where watching TV,
the sun was shining,
when the telephone rang and Mrs Miller's sister called from New Zealand.

AUFGABE 18 **S. 62**

Who was chasing the cat last Saturday / What was the dog doing last Saturday?
Who was washing the dishes last Saturday? / What was Mr Miller doing last Saturday?
Who was watching TV last Saturday? / What were the children doing last Saturday?
What was the sun doing last Saturday? / What was shining last Saturday?

AUFGABE 19 **S. 62**

While the Millers were watching TV, a burglar broke into their garage.
Grandma Elisabeth was cleaning the kitchen window when she saw an accident. She went to the phone and called the police.
Maggie was doing her homework when she heard a strange noise. She looked outside and saw the hail.

4 Zukunft

ÜBUNG 1 S. 64

1. We have tickets for the cinema. We **will see** you later.
We must go now or we **will miss** the bus.
2. Don't eat so much chocolate. You **will get** fat.
I think Manchester United **will not win** the football match.
3. Do you need sugar? Wait, I **will get** some.
You look unhappy. I **will not go**.
4. If I get a mountain bike, we **will go** on a cycling holiday.
If I don't find the way, I **will ask** a policeman.

ÜBUNG 2 S. 64

1. There will be a traffic jam in the evening.
2. John will come to the party, too.
3. I will call the police.
4. If the weather is bad, we will not play in the garden.

ÜBUNG 3 S. 65

Okay, we **will do** it right now. (3)
I'm ill. I hope my friend **will visit** me. (2)
If I meet them, I **will tell** them. (4)
Don't worry, we **will help** you. (3)
Tomorrow the weather **will be** fine. (1)
I'm sure Tim **will not be** angry. (2)

ÜBUNG 4 S. 65

I think I will / I'll travel around the world.
I'm sure I will / I'll live in a big house.
I suppose I will / I'll look like a film star.
Perhaps I will / I'll be president of Germany.

ÜBUNG 5 S. 65

We think Phil will come tomorrow.
Won't it rain?
Perhaps you will / you'll see my friend tomorrow.
If the shop opens, we will / we'll go shopping.
I will not / won't go to Simon's party.

ÜBUNG 6 S. 67

1. David **is going to meet** his father after school.
I **am going to stay** at home next weekend.
Dad **is going to do** the washing-up after lunch.
Our teacher promised: We **are going to listen** to pop songs.
2. Look at the clouds. It **is going to rain**.
Ann has got a cloth in her hand. She **is going to clean** her bike.
Aunt Helen called. Sue and Kim **are going to visit** her tomorrow.

ÜBUNG 7 S. 67

Jim has got toothache. He **is going to see** the dentist. (2)
Look here. I **am going to eat** your cookie.
We **are going to move** to Italy next year. (1)
Look at the ship. It **is going to sink**. (2)
My plans for Saturday: I **am going to do** a lot of sports. (1)
Jane **is not going to come**. She had an accident yesterday. (2)

ÜBUNG 8 S. 67

Will is going to play football on Saturday at 4 p.m.
Sandra is going to go to the lake on Sunday at 9 a.m.
Dave is going to visit Francis on Saturday at 2 p.m.
Betty is going to watch Formula 1 on Sunday at 3 p.m.
I am going to meet some friends on Saturday at 11 a.m.

ÜBUNG 9 S. 68

Pat: "Look at those clouds. It **is going to rain** soon."
Kim: "Don't worry. We **are going to reach** the next village in five minutes. So we **are not going to get** wet."
Pat: "That's not right. The next village is three miles away. And look, the first raindrops! We **are going to get** wet."
Kim: "What **are we going to do** now?"
Pat: "Look, there's a shelter. We **are going to wait** there until the rain stops."

ÜBUNG 10 **S. 68**
Look, the little girl! She is going to fall off her bike. (2)
Are you going to spend your holiday in Italy? (1)
Look at the clouds! It is going to snow. (2)
Here are the tickets. We are going to go to the open-air concert on Saturday. (1)

ÜBUNG 11 **S. 70**
will-future: wahrscheinlich eintretende Zukunft
going to-future: fest geplante Zukunft

ÜBUNG 12 **S. 70**
Ereignisse, die du nicht beeinflussen kannst → *will-future*
Du hoffst, dass etwas eintritt. → *will-future*
Ihr habt einen festen Plan für das kommende Wochenende. → *going to-future*
Du entscheidest dich ganz spontan, deinem Freund zu helfen. → *will-future*
Du beobachtest zwei Autos, die gleich zusammenstoßen werden. → *going to-future*
Wenn du Arzt bist (Bedingung), dann wirst du Leben retten. → *will-future*

ÜBUNG 13 **S. 70**
Randy: "Look here, my bike. I can't use it, the brakes are not working. My dad **is going to repair** it on Saturday."
Simon: "Don't wait until Saturday. I **will check** it for you."
Randy: "Thanks a lot. But I need new brakes. Dad and I **are going to buy** them on Saturday. Do you want to come with us?"
Simon: "Yes, of course, I **will come**, too."

ÜBUNG 14 **S. 71**
Are you going to watch the match on Sunday? No, I'm not.
Will Ralph like my dog? No, he won't. He hates dogs.
Will the sun shine tomorrow? Yes, it will.
What are you going to do on Tuesday? I'm not sure yet.

ÜBUNG 15 **S. 71**
Fortune teller: "You **will be** happy all your life."
Ruth: "That's nice. I **am going to have** a party next Sunday. **Will it be** a good party?"
Fortune teller: "Let's see. Yes, it **will be** good. And a nice boy **will come** to the party. His name is Andrew."
Ruth: "Yes, you are right. Andrew **is going to come**. I invited him."

ÜBUNG 16 **S. 71**
What about next Friday? – I **am going to play** basketball with my friends.
I've got a headache. – Have you? Wait here and I **will get** a glass of water for you.
Why are you filling this bucket with water? – I **am going to wash** the car.
If you take the dog for a walk, it **will not / won't bark** anymore.
It's decided, they **are going to build** a new house. It **will be** very noisy the next months.

Klassenarbeiten

AUFGABE 1 **S. 72**
Look at him, I **will help** him with his heavy bags.→ will: spontane Entscheidung
Oh no, the dog **is going to bite** her! → going to: absehbares Ereignis
We **are going to buy** a present for mum on Saturday. → going to: festes Vorhaben

AUFGABE 2 **S. 72**
Ben: "I hope we **will not / won't get** too much homework for today. What **will the weather be** like in the afternoon?"
Paul: "I think it **will be** nice and sunny in the afternoon. If we do not get a lot of homework, we **will have** time to play together."
Ben: "We can ask our teacher. I hope she **will not / won't give** us too much homework."

AUFGABE 3 **S. 72**
Mary: **"Are you going to come** to our party on Saturday? We **are going to have** a barbecue."
Sandra: "Yes, I **am going to come**. My mum **is going to get** some veggie burgers. "
Mary: **"Are you going to sleep** here?"
Sandra: "No, my mum **is going to pick** me up after the party."

AUFGABE 4 **S. 73**
If I go to Edinburgh, I **will visit** my aunt.
Are you going to buy a bike?
We **are going to have** lasagne for dinner.
I think I **will like** this work.

AUFGABE 5 **S. 73**
I am going to be a pilot.
We hope she will be happy in Australia.
Are you going to play football on Sunday?
We won't climb up the hill.
We are not going to climb up the hill.

AUFGABE 6 **S. 73**
Will she pass the test? – No, she will not / won't pass the test.
Will I be happy? – No, I will not / won't be happy.
Is Richard going to come at the weekend? – No, Richard is not going to come at the weekend.
Are you going to play together? – No, we are not going to play together.

AUFGABE 7 **S. 73**
Lösungsvorschlag:
Ein fester Plan für nächsten Monat: I am going to be nice to my brother.
Eine Vorhersage über deinen zukünftigen Beruf: I'm going to be an astronaut.
Ein festes Vorhaben für nächste Woche: I am going to write to my aunt.
Eine Vorhersage über das Wetter am nächsten Wochenende: It will be sunny.
Eine Vorhersage über deinen zukünftigen Wohnort: In 10 years I will live in Berlin.

AUFGABE 8 **S. 74**
Look at the sky. It **is going to snow** any minute now.
I think it **will rain** tomorrow.
Sally can't go out tonight. She **is going to do** her homework.
Are you going to the cinema? Wait a minute. I **will go** with you.
My dad has made up his mind. He **will stop** smoking.
If you go by train next week, I **will take** you to the station.

AUFGABE 9 **S. 74**
Penny is carrying a lot of books that are too heavy for her. She **is going to drop** some of them.
There are lot of dark clouds in the sky. It **is going to rain.**
Jack isn't careful enough and there is a man standing right in front of him. He **is going to walk into** that man.
Dave is in his classroom and he has got some chalk. He **is going to write** something on the board.
Luke is driving far too quickly. Hopefully, he isn't **going to crash** into a tree.
Look, there are two boys ice skating, but the temperatures are above zero. The ice **is going to break**.
Mrs Snyder's cat has climbed up her tree again. It's Kitty again at the top of tree. She **is going to fall down.** Poor thing. Last time the firemen had to rescue her.

AUFGABE 10 **S. 75**

Brian, I'm sure you will enjoy your stay in Wales. Maybe the weather **will be** fantastic. There are hardly any clouds. So the sun **is going to shine.**
We bought a house in York last year. We **are going to move** up north.
Do you think it **will be** cold tomorrow?
Would you like to come to Angela's birthday party? – Well, I'**ll think** about it.
Perhaps Sue **will meet** him again one day.
I'm afraid Matthew can't come tonight. He **is going to play** in an important football match tomorrow.
Kim **will have** a proper breakfast before she goes hiking.

AUFGABE 11 **S. 75**

It **will be** wet when we arrive in the Lake District.
Pete **is going to look** for a job in London.
Be careful. It is raining and there are a lot of leaves on the ground. You **are going to slip.**
Will loves travelling. He **is going to travel** for a year.
Jane's birthday **will be** on a Wednesday this year.
Wait a minute. I'**ll help** you.
If I don't go to bed early, I **will be tired** next day.
Look at this kitchen table: butter, sugar, flour. Mum **is going to make** a cake.

AUFGABE 12 **S. 75**

I'm not sure if / whether I will buy this bike.
Zoe has got tickets for a concert. She is going to go to a concert on Friday. / She is going to a concert on Friday.
Pam and Lucy are going to have a party at the weekend.
Christmas will be on a Sunday this year.
Sit down. I'll close the window.

5 Der Satz

ÜBUNG 1 **S. 77**

James gave her a present.
He can write a letter.
George and his brother were going to the shop.
Richard has painted the table.
I must change my clothes.
The Queen is going to meet the Prince of Wales.

ÜBUNG 2 **S. 78**

I often play CDs.
He sometimes listened to music in his room in the evenings.
Tina never visits her grandmother.
My father and I are going to play badminton in the park on Sunday.
Sarah went shopping in town on a fine day last week.
We are going to cook dinner in the kitchen at six o'clock.
They have always done their homework carefully.

ÜBUNG 3 **S. 78**

She bought a lot of clothes although she **didn't have much money.**
Jim was unfair so **I shouted at him.**
I opened the window because **it was so hot.**
Mrs Walker wanted to come but **she didn't know when.**
Rose likes to ski although **she broke her right leg twice.**
Mrs Craig wanted her pupils to be quiet but **they wouldn't stop talking.**
The children are playing inside because **it is raining heavily.**
The kitchen looks a mess so **I will help Mum to clean it up.**

ÜBUNG 4 **S. 78**

Last year my parents bought a house.
Fred has learned Spanish for nine years.
Philipp and Greg bought neither flowers nor another present.
Jim sometimes clears the table.
I can go to the party tomorrow.

ÜBUNG 5 **S. 80**
He was (HV) sitting (VV) on the chair.
She went (VV) to bed early.
Christina has (HV) worked (VV) for two hours.
Lydia and Kim were (HV) having (VV) fun.
He wrote (VV) an e-mail.
Tina is (HV) eating (VV) a banana.

ÜBUNG 6 **S. 80**
He was not / wasn't sitting on the chair.
She did not / didn't go to bed early.
Christina has not / hasn't worked for two hours.
Lydia and Kim were not / weren't having fun.
He did not / didn't write an e-mail.
Tina is not / isn't eating a banana.

ÜBUNG 7 **S. 81**
They didn't listen to music.
Liz didn't work in the garden.
Larry doesn't buy a present.
We didn't watch TV.
I didn't clean the windows.
She doesn't read the book.
They don't go to the museum.

ÜBUNG 8 **S. 81**
Tino did not / didn't go home yesterday.
Nobody ate the cake. Walter and Ian were not / weren't taking the bus.
Rita is not / isn't going to meet Tina.
They have never read a book.
Janice did not / didn't help her mum.

ÜBUNG 9 **S. 82**
Mum cannot / can't cook.
I did not / didn't jump on the chair.
She has not / hasn't read a book for two weeks.
Charly need not / needn't go home soon.
It will not / won't rain today.
Freddy is not / isn't going to sing for us now.
Nobody sang a song.
I have not / haven't gone to school yet.
They may not know it.
They have never been to France.
They will not / won't come.

ÜBUNG 10 **S. 84**
If Kim **visits** Tom, she **will have** a good time.
If our team **wins** the match, we **will have** a big party.
If it **rains**, Tim and Gina **will go** by bus.
Mr Jones **will catch** the 7:15 train if he **leaves** immediately.
If they **visit** Aunt Jill, they **will see** the picture.
My parents **will sell** our old car when they **buy** a new one.
If Simon **writes** her an e-mail, Tina **will be** happy.
If you **eat** too much chocolate, you **will feel** bad.

ÜBUNG 11 **S. 84**
If I tell you the truth, you will be shocked.
If you don't call her, she will be angry.
If Susan stays longer, she will miss the bus.
If you go to bed early, you will not / won't be tired the next morning.
If we work hard, we will get good marks.
If he doesn't do his homework, he will not / won't pass the exams.

ÜBUNG 12 **S. 85**
Mum **will be** there **if** you **arrive** at 7 o'clock.
When we **start** eating, you **will not / won't be** hungry anymore.
Sally **will read** the book **when** she **gets** it.
Henry **will win** the match **if** Sandy **doesn't play** well.
When she **arrives** at the hotel, **she will** meet him.
If you **make** too many mistakes, you **will not / won't** pass the exam.

ÜBUNG 13 **S. 85**
I will go home when it gets dark.
My mother will be angry if I do not / don't come.
Mr Jordan will feed the dogs when we ask him.
Simon will not / won't do the shopping if his mother doesn't ask him.
When / If Tina reads the message, she will be unhappy.

ÜBUNG 14 **S. 88**
who: Personen
which: Dinge oder Tiere
that: Personen, Dinge, Tiere
whose: zeigt eine Zugehörigkeit an

ÜBUNG 15 **S. 88**
A Smart is a car **which** is small.
He is the boy **who** took the CD.
People **who** drive too fast are stupid.
These are the books **that** are cheap.
Ted, **who** found the money, is a young man.

ÜBUNG 16 **S. 89**
Frederic is a boy **who** can sing and play the guitar.
Jason's mother is a nurse **who** works at General Hospital.
They showed a film **that / which** was brilliant.
This is Margret **whose** aunt works in the bakery.
This is my friend Ron **who** bought a blue bike.
Mr Harold is the neighbour **whose** dogs are always barking.
Mrs Richard is the teacher **who** went bungee jumping last year.

ÜBUNG 17 **S. 89**
A sheperd is a person who / that looks after sheep.
A teacher is a person who / that works with children.
A VW Beetle is a car that / which looks like a beetle.
A lipstick is a pen that / which colours your lips.
Brad Pitt is an actor who / that is very famous.
A waiter is someone who / that works in a restaurant.

ÜBUNG 18 **S. 90**
1. *Who* wird als Subjekt gebraucht und kann nicht weggelassen werden. Der Satz bleibt gleich.
2. *That* wird als Objekt gebraucht und kann weggelassen werden. Der Satz lautet dann: Take the cheese I bought yesterday.

ÜBUNG 19 **S. 90**
This is the key ~~which~~ I was looking for.
Teresa helped grandma who was in hospital.
Mrs Rose is the teacher ~~who~~ Francis had in biology.
Take the shirt which is in the washing machine.
Take the cup ~~which~~ you like most.
Where is the CD ~~that~~ I got for my birthday?
This is the watch which is broken.
Luke likes the book ~~which~~ he has just read.
Anna loves the boy who sits next to her in class.
My father is a man who collects stamps.

ÜBUNG 20 **S. 91**
Jane Austen is a British author who wrote a lot of novels.
Volleyball is a team sport young and old people like.
I like people who / that are happy.
Justin is a boy you can trust.
It's Jim's box Linda found last week.
Marion loves a man who / that works for a big company.
Where is the pen I was using for my letter?
The car hit the tree which / that was lying on the street.

ÜBUNG 21 **S. 92**
Can you see **the bike which** is in front of the shop?
This is **the man who** helps me with my homework.
This is **the homework which** I couldn't do.
Is this **the singer whose** CDs you like?
Have you got **a knife which** is sharp enough for the bread?
Peter is **my cousin who** lives in Peru.
These are **the Millers whose** daughter sings in a famous choir.
They stole **Janet's purse which** was in her jacket.
Is this **the dog whose** bark is worse than its bite?
Look at **those women who** are dancing over there!

ÜBUNG 22 **S. 92**

Gina's mother works for a company that / which produces computers.
Queen Elizabeth, who lives in Buckingham Palace, doesn't have to pay the rent.
This is the old CD that / which was in my bag.
The old man, who / that is sitting at the table next to us, is blind.
Babette, who is interested in art, is an old friend.

Klassenarbeiten

AUFGABE 1 **S. 93**

I have lived in Berlin for four years.
Dana did not / didn't like the show.
Francis cannot / can't start the race.
I was not / wasn't afraid of the test.
Simon is going to wash the car.
She was not / wasn't cleaning her bike.

AUFGABE 2 **S. 93**

He went to bed **because** he was tired.
You can **either** have coffee **or** tea.
Tom doesn't talk to Pam **although** he likes her.
John didn't win the prize, **but** the audience loved him.
This is **neither** my dog **nor** his dog.

AUFGABE 3 **S. 93**

We always go to the cinema on Saturday evenings.
Tim never forgets his keys.
My mother sometimes plays the piano in the evening.
We often go skiing in winter.

AUFGABE 4 **S. 93**

Frank did not / didn't clean his bike.
She was not / wasn't sitting in the bar.
Tom is not / isn't going to come.
Betty has not / hasn't seen the bird.
They did not / didn't listen to music.
I will not / won't be a film star.
Sarah has not / hasn't bought a skirt.
The police did not / didn't catch the thieves.

AUFGABE 5 **S. 94**

Kevin **will be** a good student if he **learns** more.
The cat **will fall** down if it **does not / doesn't** stop.
If we **start** now, we will **finish** at 12 o'clock.
If Sue **walks** faster, she **will not / won't** get wet.
If you **wait** for me, I **will help** you.

AUFGABE 6 **S. 94**

Is this your bike **that / which** is standing in front of the tree?
Give me the book **that / which** is on the shelf.
Can you show me the lady **whose** bag this is?
This is my brother **who / that** works at the cinema.
Mrs Johnson is the lady **whose** son lives in Canada.
Are you the boy **who / that** lives next door?

AUFGABE 7 **S. 94**

Look at the girl who is next to Peter.
Mum baked a cake you will like a lot.
Take the plate which / that is clean.
This is the friend who can juggle.
Carina is reading the book Tim was talking about.
Did you know the man who / that asked for some money?

AUFGABE 8 **S. 94**

Ruth and Kim did not / didn't talk to me yesterday.
If you repair the bike, I will cook for you.
Gina is the girl who plays basketball.

AUFGABE 9 S. 95

simple present	She often goes to school by bike.
simple past	Alan wrote letters yesterday.
present perfect	The children have eaten ice cream.
simple present	I am in a hurry.
past progressive	Clive was playing tennis.
will future	Maybe her friends will come next week.
present perfect	Mum has just come upstairs.
going-to-future	We are going to visit Aunt Beth.

AUFGABE 10 S. 95

We will meet in front of the cinema **at seven o'clock.**
The Millers **usually** go to France during their summer holidays.
Sue has **never** been to London.
Mary looked at her dog **angrily.**
We can meet **at five o'clock** on Friday.

AUFGABE 11 S. 96

I often go swimming but I never **play football.**
It was snowing yesterday so we **could go skiing.**
I have just bought those jeans although they **were really expensive.**
We had to go inside because there was **a terrible storm.**
Joe started to swim when he was five so **he can swim really well.**

AUFGABE 12 S. 96

I like dogs **which / that** don't bark or bite.
I don't like people **who / that** talk all the time.
I don't like films **that / which** are about monsters.
I like books **that / which** are about wizards and fairies.
I like friends **who / that** don't tell lies.

AUFGABE 13 S. 96

Tim gave Jane **some of his old CDs yesterday.**
Judy is waiting **for Veronica in front of the old house.**
Rick has just written **some emails to his friends.**
I'm looking **for my mobile in my room.**
I **often look for my pen.**

AUFGABE 14 S. 97

Is it okay **if** I open the window? **If** it is too cold, I'll close it at once.
When we get home, we'll have tea. I have already made the sandwiches.
Ben, you must phone us **when** you arrive in Liverpool.
I'll get you something to eat **if** you are hungry.
My parents will pick us up from Kate's house **when** we phone.
If you study for the next class test, you will get a good mark.

AUFGABE 15 S. 97

If you wait a minute, **I'll go** with you.
It will be quicker if **you go** by train.
We will go swimming if the weather **is fine**.
If I go to bed after 10 o'clock, I will oversleep.

AUFGABE 16 S. 97

Lösungsvorschlag:
If I get a good mark in my English test, **I will be happy.**
If I win the first prize in a competition, **I will have a party with all my friends.**
If I find a purse in the street, **I'll take it to the lost property office.**
If I have an accident with my bike, **I'll phone my parents.**
If I'm hungry, **I'll eat some biscuits.**
If I'm too late for school, **I'll have to find a good excuse.**

AUFGABE 17 **S. 98**

This must be the actor **who / that** Ben always talks about.
This is the bird **which / that** has a broken wing.
I don't like the shoes **that / which** Victoria is wearing.
I was angry with my friend **whose** sister was rude to me.
There is the school **where / that** I went to for four years.
Is this the part of the palace **which / that** burnt down last year?

AUFGABE 18 **S. 98**

That is the disco Robert met Sarah at.
This is the snack bar which / that is famous for its crisps.
We saw the man who lives in a huge house just across the road.
This is my uncle whose name is Billy.
Tim is a friend I can trust.

AUFGABE 19 **S. 98**

If it snows heavily, the headmaster will close the school for two days.
When school is over, most children walk to the bus stop.
Fiona doesn't know the house in which / where her friend lives/which her friend lives in / that her friend lives in.
We spent our holidays in Italy two years ago. / Two years ago we spent our holidays in Italy.
I met Sally in town at about three o'clock yesterday. / Yesterday I met Sally in town at about three o'clock.

6 Fragen

ÜBUNG 1 **S. 101**

Z	W	B	Y	J	N	W	B
W	H	O	Q	Q	G	H	V
V	E	A	E	R	F	Y	Z
X	R	S	Z	G	L	H	I
H	E	W	H	O	S	E	Z
O	U	R	R	A	O	C	C
W	H	E	N	W	B	H	J
U	M	R	H	W	H	A	T

where: wo / wohin
who: wer / wen
why: warum
what: was
when: wann
how: wie
whose: wessen

ÜBUNG 2 **S. 101**

Where were you?
Who went to school?
How were they?
Why did you like potatoes?
Whose jeans were these?
When did the shop open?
What books did you like?
Who was your favourite actor?

ÜBUNG 3 **S. 101**

Did Mum buy a book?
Was he going to school?
Were they afraid of the test?
Did you study for the test?

ÜBUNG 4 **S. 101**

Where did Jonathan go to?
Who sat on the chair?
When did he play football?
Whose bike was this?

ÜBUNG 5 **S. 102**
Did she sit in the park?
Did you help grandma?
Didn't he write an e-mail?
Were you hungry?
Did they listen to a CD?
Was he alone?
Were they old?
Did you go skating?
Were they ready?
Didn't he fly to Rome?

ÜBUNG 6 **S. 102**
1. Who visited his aunt in Birmingham?
What did Frank do in Birmingham?
Who did he visit?
Where did he visit his aunt?
2. Who saw an old lady?
What did Sandra and Jenny do?
What / Who did they see?
Where did they see the old lady?
Who looked very sad?
How did the old lady look?

ÜBUNG 7 **S. 103**
Did you take pictures? Were you taking pictures?
Didn't they play volleyball? Weren't they playing volleyball?
Did he go to the concert? Was he going to the concert?
Did you have fun? Were you having fun?
Did we buy a present? Were we buying a present?
Didn't Tim write an essay? Wasn't Tim writing an essay?

ÜBUNG 8 **S. 104**
Did he buy the green shirt? – Yes, he did. / No, he didn't.
Was she having fun all day long? – Yes, she was. / No, she wasn't.
Did they play basketball? – Yes, they did. / No, they didn't.
Was he sad? – Yes, he was. / No, he wasn't.
Were you at the party? – Yes, I was. / No, I wasn't.
Was the cat sitting next to us? – Yes, it was. / No, it wasn't.

ÜBUNG 9 **S. 104**
They weren't sitting in the kitchen, were they?
It rained in the afternoon, **didn't it**?
She didn't clean the room, **did she**?
Georgia wasn't in the hospital, **was she**?
They talked to Harry, **didn't they**?

ÜBUNG 10 **S. 104**
Who bought the shoes?
When did Jane come home?
How long has Gwen been living in Wales?
Why are you late again?
Where can I put my coat?
How often has Robert phoned so far?
Who are you going to invite to your party?

ÜBUNG 11 **S. 105**
I love to read. Have you got any books?
Tina is vegetarian. She doesn't like any meat.
Here is your tea. But I'm sorry, I haven't got any milk.
Let's have a party. I want to have some fun.
Soon it's Christmas. Have you already bought any presents?

ÜBUNG 12 **S. 105**
Verena wants to buy **some** apples.
He has lost his keys **somewhere**.
Can **anyone / anybody** help me?
Are there **any** eggs left?
She hasn't got **anything** to say.
I am wearing **something** new.
It was dark. I didn't see **anything**.
Let's make **some** sandwiches.
Where are my keys? I can't find them **anywhere**.

ÜBUNG 13 **S. 107**
Where has Kim been so far?
Who has helped Jim since April?
Why have you been to Paris?
Whose car have they stolen?

ÜBUNG 14 **S. 107**
Who has been to Russia?
What has he left at school?
Where has Mr Finn been?
Why have they slept too long?
Who has not called yet?

ÜBUNG 15 **S. 107**
Where has he travelled so far?
What has Betty just read?
Have you listened to the CD yet?
I have seen you, haven't I?
Has Richard learned Spanish for a long time?

ÜBUNG 16 **S. 107**
Have you been to Paris yet?
You haven't cleaned the kitchen, have you?
David, have you seen Clare?
Where has Fred worked so far?
Mr Keller hasn't flown to Japan, has he?
Has father already called?

Klassenarbeiten

AUFGABE 1 **S. 108**
Where have they been since July? *(present perfect)*
What did you watch on TV last night? *(simple past)*
Who called the police? *(simple past)*
When / where / why was Tina painting the room? *(past progressive)*
How long did you stay in Spain? *(simple past)*

AUFGABE 2 **S. 108**
Where were you?
Was Kim sitting next to you?
Where have you worked?
Was Mum crying?
When did they have to leave the party?

AUFGABE 3 **S. 108**
Where were they having fun?
Who sat on the chair?
What did they do?
When did Jane write the e-mail?
Why was grandpa unhappy?
Whose bike was dirty?
What was Gina playing?

AUFGABE 4 **S. 109**
Did Jack fly to Los Angeles? – Yes, he did.
Have you lived in London? – No, I haven't.
Was he selling the car? – Yes, he was.
Did the old lady call the police? – No, she didn't.
Has he read a lot of books? – No, he hasn't.

AUFGABE 5 **S. 109**
They haven't played golf, have they?
Vicky was watching the movie, wasn't she?
Zara saw a ghost, didn't she?
Jack hasn't known the thief, has he?
The policeman called the ambulance, didn't he?
Luke was stealing the bike, wasn't he?

AUFGABE 6 **S. 110**
Tony played football two years ago, **didn't he?**
Mr Smith hasn't phoned yet, **has he?**
The children were singing Irish folk songs, **weren't they?**
You didn't write those stories yesterday, **did you?**
Elaine wasn't driving to Cardiff, **was she?**
Robert and Lisa haven't been to Wales yet, **have they?**
Dad is watching TV, **isn't he?**
Peter didn't buy some milk, **did you?**

AUFGABE 7 **S. 110**
What was Tim doing yesterday afternoon?
When did Kim get up on Saturday?
What have the pupils in my class just finished?
Who has already eaten all the dog biscuits?
When did you see an exciting film?
Where were the boys swimming?
Who arrived too late?

AUFGABE 8 **S. 111**

simple past:
Was Tim nervous?
Who bought the present?
Where did she buy the present?
Did the pop star sing many songs?
present perfect:
Have they lived in Sweden?
Where has Tina been?
past progressive:
Was she reading?
Was she taking pictures?

AUFGABE 9 **S. 111**

Where did Mrs Green lose her bag?
When did the train arrive?
I told you the story, didn't I?
Did he read the book? – No, he didn't.
Did the children play in the garden?
Mr Smith didn't go to work yesterday, did he?
Who hasn't read this book yet?

7 Englisch lernen

ÜBUNG 1 **S. 113**

1. J K L – R S T – E F G – O P Q – M N O – W X Y – D E F – T U V – S T U – C D E – H I J
2. D G – T W – J M – C F – I L – O R – N Q – E H – S V – Q T – W Z – H K – B E – A D – M P – L O
3. N P – K M – C E – V X – J L – M O – B D – H J – P R – X Z – L N – Q S – U W – R T – D F – A C

ÜBUNG 2 **S. 113**

dumpling – ear: <u>Dutch</u> – <u>dweller</u> – <u>eagle</u> – edge – dualism – <u>dusty</u> – dump
headliner – heel: <u>Hebrew</u> – <u>heavy</u> – heftily – <u>headship</u> – hazard – <u>hearty</u>
meet – merrily: <u>mental</u> – meekly – medium – middle – meteor – <u>menagerie</u>
ideal – illusionist: <u>illegally</u> – illustrate – <u>idol</u> – idea – <u>idiotic</u> – <u>identical</u> – icy

ÜBUNG 3 **S. 113**

Regentropfen – raindrop, Regenbogen – rainbow
Feuerzeug – lighter, Leuchtturm – lighthouse
Fischstäbchen – fishfinger, Fischer – fisherman
Rucksack – backpack, Hintergrund – background

ÜBUNG 4 **S. 114**

gag → Witz, desert → Wüste, locker → Schließfach, nickname → Spitzname, to kneel → knien, foal → Fohlen, dormitory → Schlafsaal, chum → Kumpel

ÜBUNG 5 **S. 115**

['suːpəmɑːkɪt] → supermarket
['neɪbə(r)] → neighbour
['bʌkɪt] → bucket
['taɪmteɪbl] → timetable
['vedʒɪtəbl] → vegetable
['hedeɪk] → headache
['prɒbəblɪ] → probably

ÜBUNG 6 **S.115**

adj = adjective – Adjektiv, *n* = noun – Nomen
pl of = plural of – Plural von
vb = verb – Verb
Brit. = British – britische Ausdrucksweise
Amer. = American – amerikanische Ausdrucksweise
1/2 = erste und zweite Bedeutung

ÜBUNG 7 **S.118**

Hello, my name is Claire and I would like to talk about my school and **timetable**. I have been going to a **Grammar School** in Glasgow since last summer. My school is very big and there are about 900 **pupils**. I like it there and I have already become friendly with some of the girls. I'm in **year** 6 and I'm in the same **class** for all my **subjects**. You can learn two **languages** at my school: **French** or **German**. My favourite subjects are **Geography** and P. E., which is **Physical Education**.
The first **lesson** is at ten to nine. On Monday we have **Science** and after that **Technology** from 9:50 a.m. to 10:50 a.m. Then there is a **break** and after we have **History** and **Maths**.

Lunch is from 1:10 p.m. to 2:10 p.m. and you can buy something to eat in the **cafeteria**, or you can bring a **packed lunch**. We have **afternoon** lessons from 2:10 p.m. to 3:20 p.m.
After the afternoon lessons have finished I sometimes stay for my **clubs** – I play **badminton** every Wednesday.

ÜBUNG 8 **S.118**

Hi Max,
I think it's great that you're coming to visit me for the Easter holidays. It's about time that you come over to the UK to improve your English.
I really think you will enjoy it here and that you will like my family. Well, there's my mother Janet, my father Brian and my baby brother George. He will be two in three weeks. George is really cute, but he can also be terrible – but only sometimes. He has just learned how to walk and so he is following you everywhere you go at the moment. But you'll see when you come over.
I'm writing in English (I know I shouldn't) as my German is still so poor – that's what my teacher keeps on telling me. I think it is simply because I don't learn words regularly. Mind you – I do understand the grammar, which is so difficult, but it's not really a problem for me. However, learning words is definitely not what I'm fond of. Maybe your visit will help your English and my German!
I do hope that there will be plenty of sunshine here in London because it's more fun if we can do things outside. Hey, and don't forget your tennis racket because we must play together.
I have been playing tennis for four years now and I think you will be a super partner for me because you started about three years ago, didn't you?
See you soon,
Sam

1. right
2. wrong: Sam's mother is called Janet. He has only got one brother.
3. wrong: George is younger than Sam.
4. wrong: Sam is bad at German.
5. wrong: Sam doesn't learn words regularly.
6. right
7. wrong: Max should bring along his tennis racket.
8. right

ÜBUNG 9 **S. 119**

In 1191, King Richard went away on a crusade with his army and many horses. His brother, Prince John, ruled for him because King Richard was away for such a long time. Prince John hated his brother and wanted to become King. He wanted King Richard to die in a battle and never to come back to England again. Prince John was a very mean man. The people of England had to pay taxes for what was an expensive crusade. However, a lot of people were poor and couldn't pay those taxes. So some of them had to go to prison. There was also a group of men who decided to live in the forest, because they didn't want to pay any tax and they didn't want to go to prison. Robin Hood (whose real name was Lord Locksley) was one of them, because when he returned from the crusade he had no father, no castle and no land. He went to live in Sherwood Forest, where he formed a kind of army that fought against the Sheriff of Nottingham, who everyone hated.

King Richard went away on a crusade **in 1191**.
Prince John ruled for his brother King Richard because **he was away for a long time.**
Prince John was **a mean person.**
Robin Hood's real name was **Lord Locksley.**
When Robin Hood came back from the crusade, **he had no father and no land.**
Robin Hood and his men lived in Sherwood Forest and **he formed an army there.**

ÜBUNG 10 **S. 121**

Whose book is this? → It's mine.
What's the time, please? → It's ten o'clock.
What's for homework? → Read the text on page eleven.
How do you do this exercise? → Let me help you.
Can you play the CD again, please? → Yes, of course. But listen carefully now!
Can I work with Steven? → No, you have to work by yourself (*allein*).
Who's next? → It's Dan's turn.

ÜBUNG 11 **S. 121**

I think you are right.
What do we have to do?
I think it's not exciting, it's boring.
Read the text on page eleven.
Sorry, I have forgotten my exercise book.

ÜBUNG 12 **S. 121**

Can I go to the toilet / outside?
Can I ask a question, please?
Can you write it on the board?
I think so, too.
Is this right? I am not sure.

ÜBUNG 13 **S. 123**

menswear → Herrenbekleidung
whelp → Welpe
glow-worm → Glühwürmchen
central heating → Zentralheizung
balcony → Balkon
Indoors → im Haus, drinnen

ÜBUNG 14 **S. 123**

Jufawhety is a computer game.

ÜBUNG 15 **S. 124**

poor ↔ rich, cheap ↔ expensive, old ↔ young, thirsty ↔ hungry, to forget ↔ to remember, fat ↔ thin, to stop ↔ to start, tall ↔ short, wrong ↔ right, interesting ↔ boring

ÜBUNG 16 **S. 124**

Wortfeld „sprechen“: to say, to talk, to shout, to speak
Wortfamilie „leben“: to live, life, lively, living room
Wortfeld „Obst“: banana, kiwi, lemon, orange
Wortfamilie „Frucht“: fruit juice, fruitless, fruit salad, fruity

Klassenarbeiten

AUFGABE 1 **S. 125**

1. U V W – H I J – R S T –A B C – F G H – L M N
2. H J – E G – I K – O Q – N P – W Y – H J – R T
3. I K – C E – J L – M O – B D – L N – Q S – U W

AUFGABE 2 **S. 125**

murder – near: mystery – museum – neat – mum – mushroom – narrow
wear – white: who – why – weather – welcome – we – went – Welsh
million – mister: minor – miserable – mind – mile – minibus – mirror
early – else: emancipate – eighth – edge – earth – egg – ear – earl
lift – load: list – limit – loan – lock – light – lie – like – litter – lounge

AUFGABE 3 **S. 125**

Dir geht es nicht gut. → I am not feeling well.
Du weißt nicht, wie man ein Wort schreibt. → Could you spell this word, please?
Freitags: Du verabschiedest dich. → Have a nice weekend.
Du bist nicht einverstanden. → I do not agree with you.
Du brauchst Hilfe. → Can you help me?
Du willst, dass dein Lehrer ein Wort an die Tafel schreibt. → Could you write it on the board, please?

AUFGABE 4 **S. 126**
How do you spell this word?
I think the story is interesting / boring / funny.
You start! And then it is my turn.

AUFGABE 5 **S. 126**
1. The shop assistant in the bakery: "Would you like anything else?"
You: "No, that's all. How much is it?"
2. A tourist in your hometown: "Can you tell me the way to the town hall, please?"
You: "Yes, of course. Turn left and walk straight on. Turn right at the next set of traffic lights. The town hall is on the right side." (Lösungsvorschlag)
3. Your bike has a flat tyre. You to a friend: "Can you help me with my bike, please?"
Your friend: "Yes, of course. I wil help you fix it."
4. Your mum: "What would you like for dinner?"
You: "I would like to eat some spaghetti, please." (Lösungsvorschlag)
5. Teacher: "Have you got any questions?"
You: "No, I haven't. I understood everything."

DUDEN

ISBN 978-3-411-72142-9

ÜBUNG 9 **Höre dir Track 13 auf der CD zweimal an und kreuze die richtigen Aussagen an. Bevor du dir den Text anhörst, lies dir die Liste der Vokabeln durch, die dir helfen können, den Text besser zu verstehen.** 13

crusade – Kreuzzug
to rule, ruled, ruled – herrschen, regieren
battle – Schlacht
mean – gemein
tax – Steuern
prison – Gefängnis

King Richard went away on a crusade

☐ in 1190. ☐ in 1181. ☐ in 1191. ☐ in 1119.

Prince John ruled for his brother King Richard because

☐ he hated him.
☐ he was away for a long time.
☐ he wanted to be king.
☐ King Richard was dead.

Prince John was

☐ a nice person.
☐ a boring person.
☐ a funny person.
☐ a mean person.

Robin Hood's real name was

☐ Lord Nocksley. ☐ Earl Locksley. ☐ Lord Mocksley. ☐ Lord Locksley.

When Robin Hood came back from the crusade,

☐ he had no father and no land.
☐ his wife was dead.
☐ his friends hid in Sherwood Forest.
☐ the Sheriff of Nottingham was ill.

Robin Hood and his men lived in Sherwood Forest and

☐ he formed an army there.
☐ they built a new castle there.
☐ they climbed trees there.
☐ they killed the Sheriff of Nottingham there.

7.3 Englisch sprechen

Eine gute Methode, Englisch zu lernen, ist es, zu lesen oder Sätze nachzusprechen. Noch besser jedoch ist es, selbst aktiv zu werden.

Versuche ab jetzt, mehr Englisch zu sprechen
- im Unterricht,
- in der Pause mit deinen Mitschülern und Mitschülerinnen
- oder mit Touristen in der Stadt.

Could you repeat this, please?
Could you give me your pencil, please?

Can I help you? May I show you the way?

Nutze jede Gelegenheit zu sprechen, dann wird dir Englisch viel leichter fallen.

Tipp: Hab keine Angst vor Fehlern, denn aus Fehlern kann man lernen. Je häufiger du Englisch sprichst, liest oder schreibst, desto vertrauter wirst du mit der Sprache.

Achte auf die **passenden Zeiten:**

In diesem Augenblick Stattfindendes: *present progressive*	Tina is cleaning her bike now.
Wiederkehrendes: *simple present* (*he / she / it* → das *s* muss mit!)	Mrs Jay always works in the garden.
Vergangenes: *simple past*	I went to the cinema yesterday.
Bis jetzt Andauerndes: *present perfect*	We have learned English for two years.
Zukunft: *will-* oder *going to-future*	Henry is going to meet Astrid tomorrow.

Achte auf die **Satzstellung:**

Aussagen: Subjekt (+ Hilfsverb) + Vollverb	We (can) help in the kitchen.
Verneinungen: Subjekt + Hilfsverb + *not* + Vollverb	Tina wasn't walking home. George didn't go to the park.
Fragen: (Fragewort +) Hilfsverb (+ *not*) + Subjekt + Vollverb	Why are you singing this song? Did Dana write an e-mail? Why didn't you go to school yesterday?

ÜBUNG 10 **Verbinde jeweils eine Frage mit der passenden Antwort.**

Whose book is this?
What's the time, please?
What's for homework?
How do you do this exercise?
Can you play the CD again, please?
Can I work with Steven?
Who's next?

Read the text on page eleven.
No, you have to work by yourself (*allein*).
It's mine.
It's Dan's turn.
Let me help you.
It's ten o'clock.
Yes, of course. But listen carefully now!

ÜBUNG 11 **Bilde aus den folgenden Wörtern Sätze.**

you / I think / right / are

I think

do / have / what / to do / we

is / think / it / boring / it / is / exciting / not / I

on / read / eleven / the text / page

exercise book / forgotten / have / I / my / sorry

ÜBUNG 12 **Übersetze die folgenden Sätze. Achte besonders auf die Satzstellung! Schreibe in dein Übungsheft.**

Kann ich auf die Toilette gehen / hinausgehen?
Kann ich bitte eine Frage stellen?
Können Sie es an die Tafel *(board)* schreiben?
Das glaube ich auch.
Ist das richtig? Ich bin mir nicht sicher.

7.4 Besser lesen und verstehen

Texte lesen und verstehen ist nicht immer einfach. Oft tauchen Wörter auf, die du nicht kennst.

In the sports shop I bought a *fraghwert*. It looks like a kind of ski but it is different: It's shorter and broader, and you can stand on it with two feet.

Tipp: Um einen Text zu erfassen, ist es nicht nötig, jedes einzelne Wort zu kennen. Versuche einfach, **den Text insgesamt** zu verstehen!

What do you think is a *fraghwert*?

Dann kannst du einzelne unbekannte **Wörter aus dem Zusammenhang** erschließen.

Das Wort *fraghwert* kannst du nicht kennen, denn es ist ein Fantasiewort. Aber durch den Text weißt du sofort, dass es sich um ein Snowboard handeln müsste.

Man kann **einen Text auf verschiedene Arten** lesen:

- den Text überfliegen und sich einen ersten Eindruck verschaffen,

Es geht um *fraghwert*.

- bestimmte Information im Text suchen,
- den gesamten Inhalt erfassen und verstehen.

Ein *fraghwert* muss ein Sportgerät sein. Die Informationen über das *fraghwert* ergeben, dass es ein Snowboard ist.

Versuche einen Text wie ein Detektiv zu erschließen:

- Finde Informationen und
- versuche, einzelne Wörter nach und nach zu verstehen.

Aufgepasst: Bevor du ein Wörterbuch zur Hand nimmst, versuche erst, die Bedeutung des gesuchten Wortes selbst herauszufinden:

- aus dem Textzusammenhang,

In the supermarket you can buy vegetables, for example potatoes, tomatoes, carrots and cauliflowers. → Auch bei cauliflower muss es sich um ein Gemüse handeln (Blumenkohl).

- durch ein schon bekanntes ähnliches Wort aus der Wortfamilie,

Du kennst das Wort ***friend***, das unbekannte Wort *friendship* könnte also *Freundschaft* bedeuten.

- durch die Ähnlichkeit mit einem deutschen Wort.

comfortable → komfortabel, bequem

ÜBUNG 13 **Versuche die Bedeutung der folgenden Wörter herauszufinden, ohne ein Wörterbuch zu benutzen.**

menswear		whelp	
glow-worm		central heating	
balcony		indoors	

ÜBUNG 14 **Du musst nicht jedes Wort verstehen, um den Inhalt eines Textes zu erfassen. Versuche bei der folgenden E-Mail herauszufinden, was das unterstrichene Wort bedeutet.**

Dear Jack,
You have to get Jufawhety! It is so exciting. My brother put the CD-ROM in his computer and played Jufawhety all day. I had to wait three hours until I could test Jufawhety, too. It's about a castle. You have to find the way to the treasure chamber (Schatzkammer) with lots of gold and diamonds. Jufawhety is fantastic. If you want, you can borrow it sometime from me.
Write back soon!
Yours, Tom

Jufawhety is:

WISSEN

Wortfelder und Wortfamilien Ein **Wortfeld** umfasst Wörter, die dem Sinn oder der Bedeutung nach zusammengehören.	Wortfeld „sich fortbewegen“: to go, to run, to jump, to jog, to ride Wortfeld „Verkehrsmittel“: car, bike, motorcycle, train, plane
In einer **Wortfamilie** sind Wörter gleicher Herkunft enthalten.	Wortfamilie „tanzen“: to dance, dancer, dance hall, dance floor Wortfamilie „schlafen“: to sleep, sleeping bag, sleepy

ÜBUNG 15 In dieser Wortschlange befinden sich zehn Gegenteilpaare. Finde sie heraus. Achte auf die Verben im Infinitiv (mit to)!

big ↔ small

ÜBUNG 16 Hier sind verschiedene Wortfamilien und Wortfelder durcheinandergeraten. Ordne die einzelnen Wörter den richtigen Boxen zu. Benenne das Wortfeld bzw. die Wortfamilie.

to shout – lemon – to say – life – to speak – to live – fruit juice – living room – banana – to talk – orange – fruitless – to shout – fruit salad – lively – fruity – kiwi

ÜBEN

Klassenarbeit 1

60 Minuten

AUFGABE 1 **Alphabettraining – Trage die passenden Buchstaben ein.**

1. Trage den Buchstaben davor und danach ein!

   V I S B G M

2. Wie heißt der übernächste Buchstabe?

   H E I O N W H R

3. Wie heißt der vorletzte Buchstabe?

   K E L O D N S W

AUFGABE 2 **Im Folgenden stehen die beiden Leitwörter einer Seite im Wörterbuch. Markiere die Wörter, die dazwischenpassen.**

murder – near: mystery – museum – neat – mum – mushroom – narrow
wear – white: who – why – weather – welcome – we – went – Welsh
million – mister: minor – miserable – mind – mile – minibus – mirror
early – else: emancipate – eighth – edge – earth – egg – ear – earl
lift – load: list – limit – loan – lock – light – lie – like – litter – lounge

AUFGABE 3 **Verbessere die durcheinandergeratenen Sätze und trage sie hinter die passende Situation ein.**

feeling / well / I / not / am
nice / have / weekend / a
help / can / me / you
word / spell / could / you / this / please
with / agree / you / I / do / not
you / write / it / please / on / board / the / could

Dir geht es nicht gut. → .

Du weißt nicht, wie man ein Wort schreibt. → .

Freitags: Du verabschiedest dich. → .

Du bist nicht einverstanden. → .

Du brauchst Hilfe. → .

Du willst, dass dein Lehrer ein Wort an die Tafel schreibt. → .

AUFGABE 4 **Übersetze die folgenden Sätze.**

Wie buchstabiert man dieses Wort?

Die Geschichte ist interessant / langweilig / lustig.

Du fängst an. Und dann bin ich an der Reihe.

AUFGABE 5 **Englisch im Alltag – finde die richtige Frage oder gib eine passende Antwort.**

1. The shop assistant in the bakery: “ ”
   You: “No, that’s all. How much is it?”
2. A tourist: “Can you tell me the way to the town hall *(Rathaus)*, please?”
   You: “ ”
3. Your bike has a flat tyre *(Reifenpanne)*. You to a friend: “ ”
   Your friend: “Yes, of course. I will help you fix *(reparieren)* it.”
4. Your mum: “What would you like for dinner?”
   You: “ ”
5. Teacher: “ ”
   You: “No, I haven’t. I understood everything.”

TESTEN

Stichwortfinder